Harriette R. Shattuck

The Woman's Manual of Parliamentary Law

Harriette R. Shattuck

The Woman's Manual of Parliamentary Law

ISBN/EAN: 9783337155049

Printed in Europe, USA, Canada, Australia, Japan

Cover: Foto ©Suzi / pixelio.de

More available books at **www.hansebooks.com**

THE WOMAN'S MANUAL

OF

PARLIAMENTARY LAW

WITH PRACTICAL ILLUSTRATIONS ESPECIALLY
ADAPTED TO WOMEN'S ORGANIZATIONS

BY

HARRIETTE R. SHATTUCK

TWENTY-FIFTH THOUSAND
REVISED AND ENLARGED

BOSTON:
LOTHROP, LEE & SHEPARD CO.

PREFACE

————

THE Woman's Manual aims to supply the long-existing demand for an elementary book wherein the first principles of parliamentary law are so clearly set forth that *she* "who runs may read."

There are at present a great many women, perfectly well fitted, so far as intelligence and interest go, to share in the deliberations of any assembly, but who, through lack of knowing the technique of parliamentary law, are kept from taking active part in the many meetings that they constantly attend. Eager as listeners, wishing they dared to speak, reproaching themselves afterward for not speaking, they need only the confidence which comes from "knowing how," in order to become active, vital forces. They want to know when to rise and when to sit, how to begin to speak and how to close, how to frame a motion or a remark, how to open and close a meeting, how to meet an adverse motion, —

iii

all the minute details of presiding, of debating, of making motions, of conducting meetings.

Unlike the men, who almost from childhood have practised these little details till they have become as second nature, the majority of women spring full-grown into the arena of public debate, and must offset the lack of an early and natural training by the more laborious, but by no means impracticable, effort of middle life or even of old age. The honorable exceptions of women who do know how, as well as or better than most men, only prove the rule. This book, therefore, is written for women; for use in their clubs, unions, societies, — any organizations where it is important to know how to conduct a formal meeting.

The Woman's Manual is based upon no one authority in parliamentay law; the various authorities have been carefully studied and compared. Those procedures which seem to the author best and most useful have been selected, and are herein recommended; while the established fundamentals are carefully adapted to the needs of the women's organizations for which the book is written. Where there is a conflict of opinions, that procedure which is the fairest and simplest is recommended; and such procedure is supplemented by new ideas, — when the given difficulty has had no adequate solution elsewhere. It is presumed, moreover, that questions will be considered and decided upon their merits and not be restricted by partisan bias. Consequently, certain arbitrary forms which other writers have deemed it necessary to provide for *legislatures*, have been supplanted or modified by those which, while equally parliamentary, are believed to be more suitable for ordinary assemblies and societies.

In order to explain the elementary forms so that any one, however inexperienced, can understand and apply them, the text has been made as simple and rudimentary as possible. Illustrations are given of all the forms, so that the reader may know "how" as well as "why" a certain thing is done. The book is not rudimentary, however, in the sense that anything important is omitted, for it will be found to cover all that is necessary.

Should this manual be called in question as an authority, it can be said that the author has had an experience of nearly twenty years in the work of women's organizations as well as an opportunity for observation while assistant clerk of the Massachusetts House of Representatives, during a part of the time when her father ("Warrington") was the clerk of that body. Any one who wishes to study further is referred to Cushing's manual, Warrington's manual, Crocker's "Parliamentary Procedure," and "Reed's Rules," as the soundest and most helpful authorities. Fish's "Guide to the Conduct of Meetings" is also helpful to beginners.

In the present edition, the sections relating to seconding the motion, election of officers, the previous question and amendment, have been further elaborated, either in the text, or by means of the appendix, in which will also be found valuable matter on new points. The object in view has been to make still more clear the principles laid down in the earlier editions and to present additional information, which, in every case, has been called forth by real situations that have arisen in the author's experience in teaching classes and in helping to adjust club difficulties.

H. R. S.

CONTENTS

PART I

ORGANIZATION

PART II

MOTIONS

PART III

AMENDMENT

PART IV

THE PRECEDENCE OF MOTIONS

PART V

QUESTIONS OF PRIVILEGE AND ORDER

INTRODUCTION

In a democratic community, where all the people are responsible for good government, some knowledge of the proper conduct of public meetings is especially essential. It is not necessary, of course, for every one to become an expert parliamentarian, but certain fundamentals of parliamentary procedure should be familiar to every one who is liable to take part in a public meeting. It is particularly important that women, who are now entering public life in large numbers, shall, in order to command respect, conduct their meetings with a certain regard for forms.

Parliamentary law may be defined as those usages of legislative and deliberative bodies which, by long practice and experience, have become generally approved. Parliamentary law is not fixed and arbitrary, but, like the English common law, is in continual process of development, being changed and enlarged from time to time by such new usages as gain general acceptance; and no one authority is absolute.

As, in the common law, certain principles, from long custom, have become firmly fixed, while certain others are in process, so in parliamentary law, certain principles (chiefly fundamental) have become established, while many others are not yet settled. A new usage or interpretation may arise at any time, and, if it is generally recognized as good, it takes its place as a part of the body of the law.

Besides the general body of parliamentary law, there are, for use in the conduct of meetings, special rules which may be adopted by any society. As the written law, or statutes, of a State govern that State in preference to the common law, wherever they conflict, so the special rule of any assembly governs that assembly instead of the general parliamentary law.

Care should be taken, therefore, not to confound parliamentary usages with special rules, which (because they have not been generally adopted) are not yet embodied in parliamentary law. Every deliberative body, from a small club to the Congress of the United States, may make its own rules of procedure, and these are then binding upon itself; but such special rules are not authority for any other body. When any such special rule, having received the approval of many other assemblies and the sanction of time, becomes generally adopted, it is a part of parliamentary law.

When there is a special rule on any particular subject, this rule supersedes (for the assembly which has adopted it) the general usage on that subject. When there is no such rule, general usage governs; and the question, What is usage? is to be answered by deciding what is best, for the kind of assembly in question, in the light of the best precedents and authorities.

An illustration of the distinction between a special rule and a parliamentary usage may be helpful. In the United States Senate, there is a special rule that an appeal from the decision of the chair upon a question of order, may be laid upon the table. The general parliamentary usage is that an appeal cannot be tabled without at the same time tabling the whole subject to which the appeal and the question of order relate. The latter, and not the former, practice is parliamentary, notwithstanding the fact that so high an authority as the United States Senate has a special rule to the contrary.

Justice and *Equality* are the principles on which parliamentary law is founded ; upon these, the conduct of all meetings is based, and only by special rule can any method be practised which contradicts them.

The object of parliamentary law is the fair, orderly, and speedy transaction of business, or, as Jefferson says, " accuracy in business, economy of time, order, uniformity, and impartiality." The will of the majority is to be carried out, with due regard for the rights of the minority — the minority being protected from the *arbitrary* power of the majority. Every assembly should be governed in the democratic spirit, and any practice which allows any special privilege to one member over any other, or which limits in any way the right of full and fair consideration, should be discountenanced.

In deciding between authorities, these fundamental principles, justice and equality, are to be borne in mind, and no usage or rule of any body, however eminent, which conflicts therewith, is competent authority. The English House of Commons and the United States Congress have their own special rules (the United States House of Representatives has " tied itself up with rules," Warrington says in his manual), but these rules are not often suitable for ordinary assemblies or societies.

It is important to bear in mind, as Warrington also says, "that it is possible that some deliberative bodies have adopted rules incompatible with sound parliamentary principles," and Mr. Crocker, the latest authority, confirms this in the following words: "In the heterogeneous mass of rulings, none are entitled to be considered a part of a general system of parliamentary or assembly practice, except those founded on reason and justice."

It follows that the spirit of justice and equality, tempered by individual judgment and common-sense, is of more importance in a parliamentarian than knowledge of methods. The technique is necessary, but is secondary to the spirit. One can know so much of parliamentary forms as to practically deny parliamentary principles. A knowledge of the usual forms necessary for conducting a simple meeting is, however, essential, in order that inexperienced persons may not be outwitted by unscrupulous ones, and that all may have an equal opportunity to express their convictions.

THE
WOMAN'S MANUAL
READY-REFERENCE TABLE
FOR
PRESIDING OFFICERS

	Amended	Committed	Debated	Divided	Postponed	Post. Indef'ly	Prequestioned	Reconsidered	Tabled
Adjourn	No	No	No[1]	No	No	No	No	No	No
Amend	Yes	No[2]	Yes	Yes[3]	No	No	Yes	Yes	No
Commit (or Recommit) . .	No[4]	No	Yes	No[5]	No	No	Yes	Yes[6]	No
Division of the Question . .	Yes	No	No	No	No	No	No	Yes	No
Postpone	Yes[7]	No	Yes	No	No	No	Yes	Yes	No
Postpone Indefinitely . . .	No	No	Yes	No	No	No	Yes	Yes	No
Previous Question	No	No	Yes[8]	No	No	No	No	Yes	No
Question of Order[11]	No	No	No[9]	No	No	No	No	No	No
Question of Order: Appeal .	No	No[10]	Yes	No	No[10]	No	Yes	Yes	No[10]
Question of Privilege[11] . . .	No	No	No	No	No	No	No	No	No
Reconsider	No	No	Yes	No	Yes	Yes	Yes	No	Yes[12]
Table: Lay on, or Take from	No	No	No	No	No	No	No	No	No
Vote, by Ballot, etc. . . .	Yes	No	No	No	No	Yes	No	Yes	No
Withdrawal of Motion . . .	No	No	No	No	No	No	No	No	No

The numerals in this table refer to the notes on the opposite page.

NOTES

1. When no time for the next session has been fixed, and "to adjourn" would be "to dissolve" the assembly, this motion is debatable.

2. Certain amendments may be committed, provided final action on the main question is meanwhile deferred. Sec. 136.

3. Except the motion to amend by striking out and inserting, which is indivisible. Sec. 105.

4. The simple motion to commit cannot be amended; but motions including instructions, size of committee, etc., may be amended. Sec. 133.

5. Except the motion to commit with instructions, which is indivisible. Sec. 135.

6. But not after the committee has got to work. Sec. 133.

7. That is, the day, or hour, may be amended. Sec. 128.

8. For a limited time, debate being strictly confined to the previous question, excluding the main question. Sec. 57.

9. Remarks may be permitted, at the discretion of the chairman; but there is no *right* of debate, unless there is an appeal. Footnote to Sec. 153.

10. An appeal cannot be committed, postponed or tabled by itself. The whole matter out of which the appeal arose is included. Sec. 156.

11. But any motion which arises of necessity out of these questions is open to the same action as any independent motion. Secs. 149 and 153.

12. The motion to reconsider, being tabled, cannot be taken from the table. The question is settled.

REVISIONS

Certain minor changes should now be made in the Woman's Manual. These are as follows: —

Page 38. Add: "It has been decided by the United States Supreme Court that the ascertained *presence* of the requisite number establishes the quorum, whether or not they respond to the roll-call."

Page 65. Omit "In precedence, 'to divide' ranks with 'to amend.'"

Page 91, line 18. Strike out sentence beginning "After"; in-sert "These same motions (except 'to lay on the table') may also be made after the previous question is ordered."

Page 95, line 16. Strike out "debated for a limited time"; insert "undebatable." Also, after ' reconsidered," add "provided this is done before the time has expired."

Page 110. Omit "and not amendable."

Page 116. Strike out first two sentences of sec. 82; insert "The debate upon reconsideration reopens the main question for debate. It may be limited by special rule."

Page 119. Omit sentence in brackets. Also, in sec. 85, after "lay upon" add "and take from"; omit "for the previous question"; omit "appeals."

Page 123. Omit "for a limited time."

Page 180, line 16. Omit "When the previous question has been ordered." Omit same words in summary, page 186.

Page 181. Strike out lines 3 to 9 inclusive; insert " When the time for the next meeting has not been fixed, this motion precedes the motion to adjourn, and is undebatable; when the time is fixed, it is debatable, and has no such right of precedence."

Page 188. Omit the last complete sentence.

Page 219. Omit "they take precedence of all motions, are always in order."

Page 220. Strike out sentence which begins on page 219. Strike out sentence beginning: "Since" and ending on page 221. Insert "A question of order precedes *everything*, provided it strictly relates to the matter immediately pending; a question of privilege is preceded by the *undebatable* motions to fix the time and to adjourn." Change summary to correspond.

Page 230, line 22. Strike out "of these"; insert "dependent."

Page 231, line 20. For " 1 " read " 3 "; for " 2 " read " 1 "; for " 3 " read " 2."

Page 241, line 16. Omit "or reconsidered."

Page 247, line 20. Omit "to decide, etc."; line 23, omit "for the previous question."

Page 273, line 9. Omit "of privilege or."

Page 274. Omit line 21.

Page 281, line 25. Omit "or reconsidered." **Omit line 31.**

PART 1

ORGANIZATION

CHAPTER I

HOW TO ORGANIZE A TEMPORARY MEETING

THE NEED OF METHOD; THE THREE KINDS OF ORGANIZATION; THE CALL; CALLING TO ORDER; ELECTION OF CHAIRMAN; MORE THAN ONE NOMINEE; SECONDING THE NOMINATION; ELECTION OF SECRETARY; THE COMMITTEE MEETING.

1. **The Need of Method.** A meeting is properly conducted when it is organized by the choice of a presiding officer and a secretary, and when the matters which it is to consider are regularly presented, debated, and voted upon. Not only are discord and misunderstanding liable to arise, from a neglect of correct methods in the conduct of meetings, but the business done is imperfect, and perhaps illegal. As an illustration of "how not to do it," let us take a company of inexperienced ladies, appointed as a committee to decide some matter, or to make some arrangement. They

3

sit in a circle, with no organized chairman; they all talk whenever they please, and to one another; they do not address the chair, make motions, or take votes; one member, stemming the tide occasionally, will say, "Well, then, I suppose that is settled;" or, "Mrs. B., will you attend to that?" —and so the disorderly session goes on. Such a meeting may accomplish its object, but how much better than this chaotic fashion is the method of those other societies of women that carry on their meetings "decently and in order," and who, at the same time, learn how to conduct those larger assemblies into which they are now rapidly entering!

2. **The Three Kinds of Organization.** There are three sorts of organizations that need to be considered: the temporary meeting, for a special purpose; the committee meeting, appointed by a superior body to decide or perfect matters for that body; and the permanent organization, formed for a definite object. The difference between these three is that the first and second are temporary, and the third is permanent; also, that the first and third are independent, while the committee is a dependent body.

The only essential difference in organizing the three is, that in the committee meeting a secretary, although useful, is not absolutely necessary, the chairman having authority to act in that capacity. The permanent organization is subject to the same forms as the other two, and, in addition, must have permanent officers, duly elected, a plan of work in the form of a constitution or by-laws, a regular time of meeting, a stated purpose, and a quorum.

3. **The Call.** A meeting is called by any person or persons interested, by means of verbal or written invitations, or by a public call in the newspapers.

Let us suppose that Mrs. Allen, Mrs. Burns, and Miss Sawyer have caused a notice to be printed in the *Mendon Telegraph*, over their signatures, as follows : —

All women who are interested in helping the sufferers by the great flood in Johnstown, are invited to meet at the house of Mrs. Alice M. Rice, 174 Blank Street, on Tuesday, October 14, at 2.30 P.M., to consult as to the best means of accomplishing this object.

(Signed)   LUCY B. ALLEN.
            DEBORAH BURNS.
            IDA F. SAWYER.

4. **Calling to Order.** The day has arrived, and nineteen ladies are present. Mrs. Rice has

arranged the chairs in lines across the room, as they would be in a hall, and, facing them, a small table and chair for the presiding officer. They wait a while for the tardy ones, and then Mrs. Allen, whose name stands first on the call, rises in the place where she happens to be, if necessary she raps to secure attention, and says: "Friends, the time to which our meeting was called has more than arrived. Will you please come to order and nominate some one as chairman of the meeting?" She remains standing, and waits for nominations.

If Mrs. Allen is absent, or does not wish to call to order, any one else may do it, preference being given to those who signed the call. If the meeting has been called by private invitations, any one present may call to order. The "lady of the house" has no special privileges, and, indeed, it is better for her not to call to order, or to preside, since she is usually occupied with her duties as hostess.

5. **Election of Chairman.** Miss Lovell, rising and looking at Mrs. Allen, says: "I nominate Mrs. Burns as chairman." She does not address Mrs. Allen as "Mrs. Chairman," because she is not regularly a chairman, but only a self-constituted

one. Miss Lovell sits, and Mrs. Sanders rises and says : " I second the nomination " [*sits*]. Mrs. Allen then says : " Mrs. Burns is nominated as our chairman, and the nomination is seconded. Are there any other nominations ? [*she waits.*] Or any remarks ? [*waits.*] If not, those in favor of Mrs. Burns serving us as chairman will say ' Aye.' [*All those present who are in favor then respond 'Aye.'*] Those opposed, ' No.' [*Those opposed, respond 'No.'*] It is carried, and Mrs. Burns is elected chairman of this meeting " [*sits*].

In this illustration, it is supposed that Mrs. Allen believes that the majority have answered " Aye." If, on the contrary, it seems to Mrs. Allen that there are more " Noes " than " Ayes," she says : " It is lost, and another nomination is in order." Some one will then nominate another person in the same way.

6. **More than One Nominee.** It is always well, before putting a name to vote, to ask, " Are there any other nominations ? " thus saving the meeting from hasty action, or from having a chairman forced upon it by " cut and dried " proceedings. In the illustration, if some one had desired

another than Mrs. Burns for chairman, that person would rise and say, "I nominate Mrs. Robbins;" and still another could say, "I nominate Miss Sawyer," and so on, Mrs. Allen meanwhile waiting till all had nominated who wished. Then she would put the names to vote, one by one, beginning with Mrs. Burns as the one first mentioned, and if she were defeated, going on with the other names, in the order nominated, till one of them was elected. The merits of the candidates may be discussed until the voting begins, though this is rarely done. If Mrs. Allen is herself nominated, she puts the question upon her own name as if it were that of some one else. She is, for the time being, not "Mrs. Allen," but the agent of the meeting for securing a chairman. After the nominations are all in, the election can be by ballot, if so voted. See page 261.

7. **Seconding the Nomination.** It is well for nominations to be seconded, as this shows that more than one person is in favor of the nominee. If other nominations are asked for, however, the seconding is not imperative. The acting chairman may use her discretion in the matter.

8. **Election of Secretary, etc.** Mrs. Burns,

having been elected chairman, rises, goes to the table facing the audience, stands behind it, raps if necessary, and says: "The first business is the election of a secretary. Will you please nominate?" She remains standing, and waits. Mrs. Robbins rises and says, "Mrs. Chairman" [*this is called "addressing the chair"*]. The chair responds, "Mrs. Robbins" [*this is called "recognition," and entitles the one recognized to the floor*]. Mrs. Robbins then "has the floor," and proceeds to say, "I nominate Miss Lovell for secretary." She sits. Mrs. Preston rises and says, "I second the nomination, Mrs. Chairman."[1] The chair waits, or asks for further nominations, and then proceeds in the way already given for the election of chairman.[2] Miss Lovell, being elected, takes her seat at the table beside the chairman, is provided with writing materials, and proceeds to write down, correctly and exactly, the proceedings which have already taken place, and all that follow. She does not record

[1] The title "Madam" (chairman or president) may be used instead of "Mrs.," but it is rather fastidious to insist upon it. "Mrs." means simply "Mistress," and applies to all women, whether they are "Mrs." or "Miss."

[2] When the regular chairman or secretary of a permanent organization is absent, a temporary officer is elected in this same way.

what is *said*, put makes a full record of what is *done*, or decided by vote. She should make no personal comments.

The chairman then states the object for which the ladies were called together, making an address of any reasonable length, or saying briefly something like this: "Our meeting is now ready to consider the matter for which we have been called together. As you know, our object is to consider in what way (if in any way) we women of Mendon can help the sufferers by the terrible flood in Johnstown. Any suggestions or remarks are now in order, and the chair hopes that all present will freely express their opinions so that we may arrive at some action as speedily as possible." She then sits, rising again whenever any person "addresses the chair," and sitting during remarks. She also rises to state and to put motions, to state facts, or whenever it is necessary for the order and dignity of the meeting. The temporary meeting is now "organized" and ready for work.

9. **The Committee Meeting.** A committee meeting is organized in the same way, except that a secretary may be omitted. If the body by which

the committee is appointed has definitely elected a certain person as its chairman, that one is the chairman; otherwise, a chairman is elected by the committee at its first meeting. The mere fact of a person having been appointed first, or nominated first, on a committee, does not constitute her its chairman, except for the purpose of summoning the others to the first committee meeting. The rules for proceedings in committees are considered in chapter eighteen.

SUMMARY

A temporary meeting is organized by the choice of a chairman and a secretary; a committee meeting by the choice of a chairman; and a permanent society by the election of permanent officers and by the adoption of a constitution and by-laws.

Any person present may call a temporary meeting to order, preference being given to those who issued the call for it.

Temporary officers are chosen by nomination from the floor, the chair giving opportunity for as many nominees as are desired.

Names are voted upon one by one in the order nominated. Or, if so voted, a ballot is taken.

The temporary chairman, when elected, takes her place, and receives and puts to vote nominations for secretary.

The secretary records all that it is voted to do. She makes no comments.

A committee is organized in the same manner as a temporary meeting, electing its chairman unless one has been specified when it was appointed. Its chairman may act as secretary also.

CHAPTER II

HOW TO FORM A PERMANENT SOCIETY

FORMING A CLUB; CONSTITUTION AND BY–LAWS; THE OFFICERS; ROTATION IN OFFICE; ELECTION OF OFFICERS; OTHER METHODS OF ELECTING; "NO CHOICE;" MAJORITY *vs.* PLURALITY; CONCLUSION OF ORGANIZATION.

10. **Forming a Club**. The first meeting of any proposed permanent society is organized in the same way as a temporary meeting. It is then necessary to adopt a plan of organization, in the

form of a constitution, or by-laws, or both; and to elect permanent officers.

Illustration : Let us suppose that the same women of Mendon, having enjoyed meeting together while helping the Johnstown sufferers, decide that it will be profitable to form a permanent society or club, for social, literary, or philanthropic purposes. They call their friends together and organize their temporary meeting as already described.

Mrs. Burns and Miss Lovell having been elected temporary chairman and secretary, and the chairman having stated the object of the meeting, informal remarks are made by those present, favoring or disapproving the project. Mrs. Allen then rises, "addresses the chair," is "recognized," and says: "I move that a woman's club be formed, and that we take the necessary action at this meeting." The chair repeats the motion, it is regularly debated, and when all have spoken who wish, the motion is "put to vote,"[1] and if the majority vote in favor, the motion is carried, and the chair says, "The motion to form a club is decided in the affirmative." Technically speaking, the ladies

[1] See Chapter V. for forms for making and putting motions.

have voted to turn the present temporary meeting into a permanent organization, it being understood that all present, after fulfilling the requirements to be agreed upon, are entitled to membership in the club.

The chair, having declared the result of the vote, asks: "What further action will the club take toward perfecting its organization?" Mrs. Sanders, having properly obtained the floor, moves "that a committee of three be formed to frame a constitution and by-laws." This motion is stated, discussed, and put to vote; if carried, the chair asks, "In what way shall that committee be chosen; from the floor, or by the chair?" Mrs. Rice moves "that it be appointed by the chair,"[1] or, "that it be nominated from the floor." If the former motion is made, it is put to vote, and, if carried, the chair names three persons present, saying, "The chair will appoint as this committee,

---

[1] The custom of calling out "By the chair" or "From the floor" is incorrect, though by general consent it may be allowed. A chairman may disregard such irregular calls, and insist upon a motion regularly made. In case she allows them, she should not assume such calls to be the sense of the meeting, and act upon them without a vote, but should consider them as a motion, and put such motion regularly to vote. It is better to insist upon a proper motion.

Mrs. Robbins, Mrs. Rice, and Miss Lovell." If the other motion is made, that is put to vote instead, and, if carried, the chair asks for and receives nominations for the members of the committee, and puts them to vote, as already explained in the choice of chairman.[1] *See sections 6 and 15.*

In the same way, a motion is made and put "that a committee be formed to prepare a list of permanent officers for the club," or, "that we proceed to receive nominations for permanent officers." If a committee is appointed, that committee may retire at once, deliberate, and report a list of officers (other business being done in the meantime), or it may report at a subsequent meeting; it may also be instructed to prepare written or printed copies of its report, to be used as ballots.

The committee on the constitution and by-laws necessarily reports at a later meeting.

This is all the business absolutely necessary to be done at this initial meeting. Having thus organized temporarily, and taken steps toward permanent organization, the first meeting decides

[1] See Appendix.

upon the time and place for its next session, and adjourns.

11. Constitution and By-Laws. The committee appointed at the first meeting "to frame a constitution and by-laws" meets and prepares its report in writing. At the next meeting of the club, the first business, after the approval of the records, is the report of this committee. The report is called for by the presiding officer, and read by the chairman of the committee. The whole is read first, in order to give the club a general idea of its scope. Then the constitution is taken up and read section by section, each section being thoroughly discussed, and amended if necessary. After the first section is considered sufficiently, the chair will say, "We will now pass on to the next section," and so on, until all the sections have been considered. The chair will then say, "The question now is upon the adoption of this constitution as the constitution of our society. Those in favor * * * "[1] The same is done with the by-laws. *See Section 113.*

---

[1] Where these * * * are used, it is supposed that the reader will supply the forms necessary to complete the motion.

A model is given in the Appendix which will serve
as a basis in preparing the plan of organization for
any society. It should include the name and object
of the society, the number and the duties of its
officers and standing committees, its conditions of
membership, authority in parliamentary law, quorum, provision for amendment, and any other matters essential to an understanding of its purpose
and methods.

12. **The Officers.** The essential officers are a
president, a vice-president, and a recording secretary.
If there are to be fees, a treasurer and an auditor are
added; there may also be a corresponding and an
assistant secretary. If the business is such that it
cannot be done in business sessions consisting of the
members, directors are elected to do the business for
them. In small societies whose object is chiefly
mutual improvement rather than systematic outside
work, this object is best attained by having all the
important business presented, discussed, and finally
decided in open business meetings of the whole
society, leaving necessary details to be carried out
afterward by special or standing committees, when
ordered so to do by the whole body. Every mem-

ber thus has a voice in the management of the
society of which she is a part, the feeling of unity
and *esprit de corps* becomes strengthened, and the
spirit of justice and equality subserved.[1]

13. Rotation in Office. In societies for mutual
improvement, it is well to provide in the by-laws for
rotation in office; that is, to prescribe the term of
office beyond which certain officers may not be re-
elected. The club will thus avoid getting into a rut,
and its members will mutually share the opportunity
of learning how to conduct the meeting. This is not
equally true of societies exclusively for outside work,
because, in such organizations, there may not be
more than one or two who are sufficiently interested
to do active work, the rest simply belonging in order
to help by their fees and by the influence of their
names. In clubs for study, also, where a teacher
is at the head, strict rotation will not always be
expedient, though even here the members should
have an opportunity to learn the duties of office by
actual practice. But in ordinary women's clubs,
where the chief motive is to learn and to grow,
rotation in office is one of the best helps, because,

---

[1] See Appendix.

without it, there is danger that one or two efficient women will come to believe that they alone know what is best, and can alone manage the club. This may be true, but it is death to the growth of the rest, who, given the chance, will develop the talent that is in them, bring in new ideas and methods, and, in short, help to secure the attainment of that "mutual improvement" for which the club is seeking. Two, three, or at most four years, are long enough for any one woman to act as president, vice-president, auditor, director, or member of any standing committee. The secretaries and the treasurer being distinctively working officers, rather than executive ones, may be allowed a longer or even an indefinite term. It may be said in general, that such offices of a given society as are distinctively honorary and self-educative should be subjected rigidly to the rotation rule. Justice and equality demand that as many members as possible shall have a chance to show and to use the talent they possess.

14. **Election of Officers.** The committee appointed at the first meeting to nominate a list of officers, meets and prepares its report in writing.

At some subsequent meeting (the constitution and by-laws having been adopted) the presiding officer calls for the report of the nominating committee, and its chairman rises and says: "Mrs. Chairman, your nominating committee reports as follows: For *President*, Mrs. Alice Mayo Rice; for *Vice-president*, Miss Ida F. Sawyer; for *Recording Secretary*, Miss Ruth H. Lovell; for *Corresponding Secretary*, Mrs. Mary L. P. Robbins; for *Treasurer*, Mrs. Deborah Burns; for *Auditor*, Mrs. Frances Hall Allen," and so on to whatever other elective officers are made necessary by the constitution. She then hands the list to the chairman and takes her seat.

It will have been provided in the by-laws, whether election shall be at the same, or at a subsequent, meeting to the one at which the nominating committee reports.

If it is to be at a subsequent meeting, the chair, receiving the committee's report, says: "You have heard the report of your committee. The election of officers will take place next ——, and these names are before you as candidates." Then is the time to present other nominations, if members are dissatisfied, it being understood that the regular nominees do not exclude other nominees, though they take precedence of others.

If election is to be at once, the chair says: "You hear the report of your committee. What is your pleasure?" It is not necessary to move to "receive" or "adopt" the report.[1] Other nominations are then in order. *See the next section.*

When the time for the election comes, copies of the report are distributed (if it has been so voted) to be used as ballots; or blank slips of paper, upon which to write out their choice, will do as well, if there is plenty of time. The chairman having said "The next business is the choice of tellers," Mrs. Preston obtains the floor, and moves "that the tellers be appointed by the chair." This is put to vote, and carried, and the chair appoints Miss Anna Long and Miss Nellie Faxon. The tellers may be chosen from the floor, instead, if so voted. Each member then prepares her ballot, scratching out any name she does not like and substituting one she prefers; the committee collect the slips in a box or other receptacle, retire, count the votes, and note down the result. When they are ready,

[1] See *section* 143.

the chair, interrupting other business if necessary,
says: "Your committee on election of officers
is ready to report." Miss Long then reads the
result of the ballot, giving the whole number of
votes cast, the number necessary for a choice
(which is a majority of the votes cast), and the
number each one has received for each office as
follows: —

Whole number of votes cast	21
Necessary for a choice	11

For President: Mrs. Preston has   1

                 Mrs. Rice has   20

and appears to be elected.

For Vice-president: Miss Faxon   1

                   Mrs. Sanders   1

                   Miss Sawyer   19

and appears to be elected; and so on, to all the
offices.[1] She then hands the list to the presiding
officer, who says: "The following persons, having
received a majority vote, are elected as the officers
of this club." She then re-reads the list of offices

[1] See Appendix.

and those who are elected to fill them. This declaration of the chairman decides the matter, and the
secretary records the result. It cannot be reconsidered.

15. Other Methods of Electing. In case the
nominating committee reports at the same meeting
at which it was appointed, there will be no time to
prepare full ballots. Each officer will then be voted
for separately, on slips of paper, each member writing the name thereon, the slips being collected and
counted one by one. Instead, there may be an informal ballot, and a formal ballot afterward.[1] This
method secures freedom of choice, but takes much
more time. Still another way is for the secretary
to cast one ballot, using the nominating committee's
report as the ballot. The one ballot is then handed
to the chairman, who reads the list, declaring the
nominees to be duly elected. This method is used
far too much and is not recommended. It should
never be used, except in cases where it is certain
that all are agreed. A motion is then made "that
the secretary be empowered to cast the ballot of
the society." This motion is regularly put to vote,

---

[1] See appendix.

and if there is even one dissenting voice, it cannot be done. Such a ballot requires unanimous consent.

Another method is by nomination from the floor, either at the first or at a later meeting. This takes much time, and is a rather careless method. It is a good way only when there is danger that a nominating committee will not select persons agreeable to the majority, or to any considerable number of the members. If this method is desired, a motion is made "that we proceed to receive nominations from the floor for officers of the club. The motion is stated and debated and put to vote. If carried, the chair says : " It is a vote, and the chair awaits nominations for president." Mrs. Sanders obtains the floor and nominates Mrs. Burns, Miss Sawyer nominates Mrs. Allen, Mrs. Robbins nominates Miss Lovell. When all have nominated who wish, the chair says : " Mrs. Burns, Mrs. Allen, and Miss Lovell have been nominated for president. The members will write upon the slips of paper the name they prefer." She then appoints a committee to distribute the slips to all, and then tellers to collect. sort, and count them, the result being declared by the chair, as in the first method. The vice-president, secretaries, etc., are then nominated and elected in the same way, one by one.

Still another method is to allow members of the club, in open session, at the time the nominating committee is appointed, to rise and propose candidates for any office. These names would be merely suggestions, and the committee would be bound only to consider them, not to nominate them. A still better way would be to have a nominating committee, and to provide that an independent list of nominees may also be made by any three, five, or more persons, and that these nominees be placed upon the same written or printed list with the regular nominees. In voting, the members could then erase the name they do not want, or, as in the Australian ballot system, make a cross against the name they do want. This would secure care, freedom, and fairness, and would take less time than the former method. It should be decided upon by vote and incorporated in the by-laws which of the many various methods shall be used, and such method should be strictly adhered to.

In all cases, permanent officers should be elected
by ballot, unless it is the unanimous wish to elect
by acclamation. When this is desired, a motion is
made "to elect by acclamation;" this is put to
vote, and if there is no dissenting voice, it is done.
The names of candidates for each office are read by
the chair, one by one, the chair saying, "Those in
favor of Mrs. —— for president of the club will say
aye," as in any motion. By motion and unanimous
vote, also, the names may be all voted upon at
once, or portions of them together, instead of one
by one.

In their choice of methods, different societies
will be governed by what seems suited to their
needs, and by what is fairest. With certain societies, election may be by a nominating committee
and a printed ballot; with most, acclamation would
be too summary; with all, the method of nomination from the floor, or that of a committee and a
written ballot, could hardly fail to be impartial.[1]

16. "No Choice." If, in the case of any
office, no candidate receives a majority of the votes
cast, there is "no choice," and that officer must

[1] See Appendix.

be voted for again, as many times as are necessary, until some one is elected. For instance, in electing the president, if nineteen votes had been cast, and Mrs. Rice had received ten, Miss Sawyer seven, and Mrs. Burns two, Mrs. Rice, having a majority would be elected; but if Mrs. Rice received fewer than ten, she would not be elected, and a new vote would be taken. The chair would say: "None of the candidates for president has received a majority vote. The club will please ballot again."

17. " Majority " and " Plurality." A majority is *more than half*, a plurality is *the largest of two or more numbers.* When there are only two numbers, or two candidates, a majority and a plurality are, of course, the same; but where there are more than two, there is a distinction. In the case in question, if there had been nineteen votes cast, Mrs. Rice receiving *nine*, Miss Sawyer seven, and Mrs. Burns three, Mrs. Rice would have a *plurality*, but not a *majority*, because *ten*, and not nine, is a majority of nineteen.

A plurality, however, may elect, if it is so desired, and, if so, this should be decided by vote before the balloting begins. Otherwise, a majority elects.

In all societies, it would seem that officers ought to gain at least one more than half the votes cast, in order to entitle them to serve, so that it is better to observe the general rule of a majority vote. In elections by the people for public office, the opposite is true, the majority method having proved of great inconvenience in the States where it is used.

An election to office, once decided, is final, and cannot be reconsidered.

18. Conclusion of Organization. The permanent officers, having been elected, assume their offices at the meeting following, the temporary officials retaining their places until the close of the meeting in question.

The president, on assuming the chair, may thank the club for its confidence in her, and promise to try to carry on the business properly, and to see that the rights and privileges of the members are equally recognized and respected. She is now addressed as "Mrs. President."

The officers having been elected, and the constitution and by-laws adopted, the society is *organized* and ready for work. It is now the duty of the officers to be present and perform their several functions. But in case at any time the proper officers happen to be all absent, and the time has arrived for the meeting to be called to order, any member may call it to order, and cause a chairman and secretary *"pro tempore"* to be elected, and thus proceed to business. This is better than to keep a meeting and a speaker waiting.

A temporary and a permanent society are each governed by parliamentary usages, the former by general usage, the latter by its chosen authority. The meetings of corporations and joint stock companies (in short *all meetings*) are governed by the rules of parliamentary law, and any authority which is good for a society is equally good for these.

SUMMARY

A permanent society is at first organized temporarily, and then permanently, by election of officers, and adoption of a constitution and by-laws.

The constitution and by-laws include the name, object, and methods of the society, with the number and duties of its officers. They are prepared by a committee, and adopted, after discussion, by the whole body.

The necessary officers of a permanent organization are a president, a vice-president, and a recording secretary. Other officers may be added.

Business may be done by directors, but in societies for mutual improvement, it is better to have business meetings of the whole membership.

A compulsory change of certain officers every few years is advisable in societies for mutual improvement.

Election of officers may be by means of a nominating committee, or by nominations from the floor. All permanent officers should always be voted for by ballot. In giving the result of a vote, the number of votes against a candidate, as well as the number for, should be stated.

A majority elects, unless it is provided by vote that a plurality shall elect.

A majority is more than half; a plurality is the largest of several.

An election cannot be reconsidered.

In case of the absence of permanent officers, a chairman and secretary *pro tempore* are elected.

CHAPTER III

THE ORDER OF BUSINESS AND THE QUORUM

ROUTINE BUSINESS; THE FORMAL ORDER OF BUSINESS; "QUORUM" DEFINED; A QUORUM NECESSARY BEFORE BEGINNING; EFFECT OF "NO QUORUM" DURING PROCEEDINGS; METHOD OF COUNTING THE QUORUM.

19. Routine Business. The three formalities necessary in the conduct of meetings are the calling to order, the reading and approval of the records, and the adjournment. These constitute what is sometimes called the "routine business." Reports of standing committees may also be included under this title. The routine business, by unanimous consent, may be carried on *without formal motion and vote;* but care should be taken not to use this method with any except routine business, that is, with any except business that is merely formal, and does not call for discussion. Objection may be made by any one to its use, even in routine business.

The presiding officer of a permanent organization, when the time arrives for the session to begin, rises from the chairman's seat, stands silently a moment, raps with a gavel if necessary, and says: "The hour having arrived, the meeting will please come to order, and listen to the reading of the records of the last meeting." The secretary rises, addresses the chair [1] [*who now sits*], reads the records, and seats herself. The chair rises and says: "You have heard the records of the last meeting. Does any one notice any errors or omissions? [*she waits.*] If not, the records will stand approved. The next business is, etc."

If any one has noticed any error, she will rise and make the correction, saying something like this: "As I remember, Mrs. President, the action taken upon (so and so) was as follows:" (giving it as she remembers it.)[2] If the secretary thinks the correction is valid, and no one expresses objection, it will be made by the secretary, and the chair will say: "The records, with the necessary correction, will stand approved." If there is a difference of opinion, or if the secretary insists upon her version,

---

[1] Still better, says : " Mrs. President and members."
[2] See *section* 105.

any one may move "to amend the records in accordance with the suggestion," or, "to amend by striking
out (certain words) and inserting (others);" and
this motion is discussed and put to vote, and the
records amended or not, according as the majority
vote is affirmative or negative. The chair will then
say: "The records, as amended, will stand approved."

20. Formal Order of Business. It is well
for a society, or its president, to adopt an order
of business by which the chair shall guide its
meetings. The form is not arbitrary, but may be
something like the following: —

1. Calling to Order.
2. Reading and Approval of the Records.
3. Announcements.
4. Reports of Special Committees.
5. Reports of Standing Committees.
6. Elections.
7. Special Assignments.
8. Unfinished Business.
9. New Business.
10. Programme for the Day.
11. Adjournment.

Any society will modify this order, in accordance with its own convenience and methods. The

president arranges a list for each day, itemizing under each of these heads the special business to be brought up, and calls up each item in order. When she comes to "new business" she asks: "Is there any new business?" If there is, it is presented, disposed of, temporarily at least, and then the lecture, or other programme for the day, follows. If a special time is set for the programme to begin, all business which is not reached when this time arrives, is postponed by tacit consent till the next business meeting, unless a vote is taken "to continue the business session." The order of business, after the approval of the records, may be interrupted or changed at any point, by a motion and vote to consider any special topic.

21. **The Quorum Defined.** The quorum is that number of persons whose presence is necessary for the transaction of business. In a temporary meeting, the question of a quorum does not arise, those present, however few, constituting the meeting. In a committee, a majority of those appointed constitutes the quorum. In a permanent organization, it is necessary to provide, by rule or in the by-laws, what number shall constitute the

quorum. If it is not so provided, the quorum is a majority; and a majority would have to be present before business could be done. Less than a quorum can do nothing except to adjourn to some future date.

In legislatures, where the business is of a public nature, where it is the duty of all the members to be present, and where there is power to compel their attendance, a large quorum is expedient and just. In ordinary societies, the contrary is true. The object being to get the business done, the quorum should be fixed at a number small enough to insure that a meeting is actually held when it has been called. For a society numbering from fifty to one hundred, the quorum may well be fixed at nine; for a small society five; and for one of several hundred, fifteen or seventeen is sufficient. In fixing the quorum, the *kind* of society may also be taken into account, and if its membership, though large, is not a working membership, the quorum may be still smaller. The principle is, that *all* having the right and the opportunity of attendance, those who actually do attend, rain or shine, have the right to do the work for which they have taken the trouble to come. Absent and tardy members must take the consequences. Only as a matter of courtesy can they expect business which has been regularly assigned, to be put off because they are not present. Of course, if the members present choose, they can postpone any or all items of business and adjourn; but they need not, nor is it best to do so. If the bare quorum is present, they may go on as if there were a large meeting.

22. **Quorum Necessary before Beginning.** Whatever number is fixed upon as the quorum of any body, the presence of that number of members is necessary before any business can be done. When the time for the meeting arrives, the president counts those present, including herself, to see if the requisite number are there ; even if but one is lacking, she does not call to order, but waits until others arrive. After a reasonable time (from a half-hour to an hour), if there is still no quorum, the meeting decides to what time it will adjourn, and adjourns. The next meeting may be an "adjourned" meeting. Those present may talk over matters, but no motion, vote, or business of any

kind, is in order. It is as if the meeting had not been held. Members may be sent for to make a quorum, but they cannot be required to come. The same is true of committee meetings.

23. Effect of " No Quorum " During Proceedings. A different practice prevails where there has been a quorum, and where, during the meeting, the members have gradually departed until less than a quorum may remain. In this case, business still goes on until some one raises the point of "no quorum," the supposition being that, a quorum having been present, it is still present. Business done under those circumstances is regular, and may continue to an adjournment at the regular time. The chair is not *obliged* to note the absence of a quorum, but may continue to conduct the exercises.

If, however, any one, the chair or a member, so wishes, the question of "no quorum" can be raised and the proceedings stayed. The chair may say: "The chair calls the attention of the members to the fact that there is 'no quorum' and awaits a motion." Or, a member may rise and say: "Mrs. President, I raise the question of 'no quorum.'" Business is then suspended until the number present is counted, and if it is deficient, the meeting proceeds as in the foregoing section.

24. Method of Counting the Quorum. If the quorum is small, its presence or absence is easily ascertained by a simple count, by the president and secretary, which is verifiable by all. If it is large, it should be done by tellers or by the roll-call,[1] those recorded as present deciding the question of the presence of a quorum.

The question whether the presiding officer of a legislative assembly (whose quorum is a majority, or some very large number) may decide the question of a quorum, by himself counting those present, is still an open one. This arbitrary method may be necessary for bodies where partisan politics govern the procedure; but for all ordinary assemblies, precedent has established the roll-call as the safe and fair method of ascertaining the presence or absence of members.

In any given case where the opportunity arises,

---

[1] For the way to call the Roll see *section* 72.

the natural tendency of all presiding officers toward the assumption of autocratic power should be restricted rather than encouraged.

SUMMARY

Routine business, by general consent, may be carried on without regular motions and votes.

Meetings of permanent societies should be guided by a formal order of business, including, under suitable heads, all that will be likely to arise.

The quorum is that number of persons whose presence is necessary for the transaction of business. If the number is not stated, it is a majority of the membership. It is better to have it definitely fixed.

The quorum should be small enough to insure a meeting being held when one is called, those taking the trouble to come being entitled to do the business.

A meeting is not called to order till a quorum is present; but once in progress, it may go on without a quorum until some one raises the question of "no quorum."

The presence of a small quorum is ascertained

by a count; of a very large one, by the roll-call.

When there is shown to be "no quorum," no business can be done except to arrange for a future meeting, and to adjourn.

CHAPTER IV

RIGHTS AND DUTIES OF MEMBERS

DUTIES AND RIGHTS OF THE PRESIDING OFFICER; RIGHTS AND DUTIES OF MEMBERS; THE VICE-PRESIDENT; THE RECORDING SECRETARY; VACANCIES; REMOVALS; SPECIAL MEETINGS, ETC.

25. Duties of the Presiding Officer. The presiding officer is the servant of the whole body, not the servant of any party or individual; above all, *not the master* of the assembly over which she presides. She *directs*, by means of her order of business, seeing that all is conducted in accordance with justice and equality. She "preserves order and decorum" by calling to order when necessary, and correcting parliamentary errors, holding the reins, so to speak (but not too tightly), and guiding, not driving, the session, through its by-ways to its destination. It is her duty to be strictly non-partisan while in the chair; to see that while the will of the majority is carried out, the rights of the minority are also respected; to secure the speedy and fair transaction of business, and freedom and impartiality in debate.

A good presiding officer will have three characteristics, — force of will, sincerity of purpose, and consideration for others.

As to matters of detail, the chair will do that which best preserves order and secures the proper transaction of business. She will stand during all business or voting, especially while stating and putting motions, but may sit during debate. She will not speak of herself as "I," but as "the chair" or "the president." She will recognize the member to whom the floor rightfully belongs, will state every motion that is in order, and give a chance for its discussion; she will wait for a quorum before beginning, and will open and close the meeting at the proper time; she will know when committees are to report, and see that their reports are called for; she will see that special assignments are called up at the proper time, and that all necessary business is either done, or else properly postponed, before the meeting dissolves.

26. Rights of the Presiding Officer. The presiding officer is a member of the society or meeting, and as such may always vote and speak. These rights are usually waived, however, except in cases of necessity. The chairman may make explanations or state facts, but if she wishes to debate, she leaves the chair (saying, "Will Mrs. —— please assume the chair?") and becomes merely a member for the time being. She need not actually vacate the real chair, though in large assemblies she simply assumes that another person is the chairman, and then "addresses the chair" as a member, and goes on with her remarks, resuming her chairmanship at their close.

The chair has the right to decide who is entitled to the floor, and to decide points of order, both of these being subject to appeal. She may call up regular business without waiting for motions; if there is no objection she may declare certain routine business "approved" without a formal vote, and adjourn a meeting when it is time. She may require motions to be put in writing, and may re-fuse to put those that are not in order.

A president has no right to meet with a committee, unless she has been specially appointed upon it, and she need not be consulted by members of it. She has no so-called *ex officio* rights, unless these are specifically granted, and it is not well to grant them. Her rights consist, not in managing the society, but in directing it so that it may manage itself.

27. **Rights and Duties of Members.** The members will best do their duty in assisting the president to preserve order, by preserving order themselves. They will refrain from whispering, from "asides," from walking about, from doing anything which may distract the meeting and prevent others from speaking and listening. They will make motions properly, debate courteously, and abide by the voice of the majority. Every member is upon an equality with every other. It is the right of members to vote, and also their duty, when clear as to their convictions. The rights and duties of members in debate are considered in chapter seven.

28. The Vice-President and the Secretary.
The vice-president is the substitute for the president in case of her absence or disability. Her
duties are the same therefore, and she should inform herself upon the objects and methods of the
society, and upon parliamentary practice. It is
well for a president to call often upon her vice-
president to aid her in different ways, so that the
latter office shall not degenerate into a sinecure.

The recording secretary records at the time, and
afterward writes out in permanent form all that is
done, but need not record what is said, unless
so instructed. Votes are to be transcribed in the
exact form in which they are taken. The record
is the authority; whatever that says, stands as
the legal acts of the society. It is necessary,
therefore, that the records of a meeting be read
at the meeting subsequent, and be then "approved"
by motion and vote of the society, or by tacit consent. They are thus sanctioned as correct; and it
is these records, and not the memory or assertion
of any individuals, which decide what the action
has been. Rejected motions must be recorded.

The secretary notifies committees of their ap

pointment, takes charge of matters which have been
tabled or postponed, and sees that they are kept in
proper shape; in short, she assists the president
in keeping matters straight. If a secretary has
made errors in her record, and the record has been
"approved" with the errors still in it, these errors
must be proven by the person asserting their presence, to the satisfaction of the majority of the
association, the assumption being that an approved
record is correct. To correct the record before it
is "approved" is therefore very important. The
secretary has no right to alter her record after its
approval. She signs each record "*So and So,
Secretary.*" If it is not already in proper shape,
she arranges and copies it at some future time. It
is best, however, to write it out at first in a record-
book, rather than upon sheets of paper. The
corrections are then made by interlining and erasure, and there is no copying to be done. Nothing that has been actually voted can be expunged
from the records except by unanimous consent.
See Appendix to *section* 87. The duties of other
officers should be specified in the by-laws of the
society which elects them, and will be determined

by the needs of that society. Every officer is to attend to her own duties; she is not to interfere with, or to be subjected to interference from, the other officers. In general, it is the duty of the recording secretary to record, and of the corresponding secretary to correspond; and whatever naturally comes under these heads belongs to these officers respectively. Any other duties may be specially assigned to either of them, or their duties may be differently divided, by vote or special rule. The president should oversee all, but not interfere, except when necessary to keep the proceedings correct. She should not be given too much power, and should be careful not to presume upon the powers which are given her.

29. **Vacancies, Removals, Special Meetings, etc.** If vacancies in office occur during the period when the society is in session, they are best filled by a new election at the earliest feasible date. If they occur during the vacation, they may remain unfilled till the society reassembles, or provision may be made in the by-laws for filling them in some other way. It is doubtful whether directors should be given power to fill their own vacancies.

Committees may well do so, as they are temporary. A vacant office is best filled by a *pro tempore* officer until a new election can be had. The duties of such an officer cease as soon as the regular officer is chosen.

Officers who become grossly negligent, or who disgrace the society, may be removed by a majority vote, which should be taken by ballot upon a motion (seconded) "that the office of —— be declared vacant." It is obvious that only in a most extreme case should this be done, the better way being to wait for the term to expire. Rotation in office best meets this difficulty.

The authorities of an organization are: *first*, its own constitution and by-laws, which are paramount; *second*, any special rules that it has adopted, or votes that it has passed, which are unlimited, except that they cannot conflict with its constitution and by-laws; *third*, its chosen authority in parliamentary law; *fourth*, general parliamentary usage. These take precedence in their order.

It is presumed that the members of a permanent organization know the place and time of regular meetings, and notification of these is not compul·

sory. With special meetings it is different. Every member must be notified of these in some regular way, prescribed by vote of the organization, and such rule must be strictly enforced. At any regular meeting, a quorum being present, any vote may be passed which does not conflict with the constitution and by-laws or with previous votes. *Per contra*, the business to come before a *special* meeting must be specified in the "call" or notice thereof, and no business except such as is thus specified can be done at such special meeting, unless all the members are present, and all agree to bringing it up. In a special meeting, more than ordinary strictness must be exercised in admitting amendments. Those which are germane are in order, as in a regular meeting, but, in case of doubt, as Mr. Crocker says: "A conservative course should be adopted with reference to admitting any amendment which materially enlarges the scope of the proposition as stated in the call." It is better to have as few special meetings as possible. They are for emergencies.

SUMMARY

The presiding officer is the servant of the whole body; it is her duty to be strictly non-partisan, to preserve order, and to guide the meetings by the rules of parliamentary law, and by an order of business.

It is the right of the presiding officer to vote and to speak, leaving the chair for debate. She has no *ex officio* rights not specifically granted.

The duty of the members is to help to preserve order and to observe the rules of procedure. They are all upon an equality.

The recording secretary keeps a correct record of all that is decided by vote. The records are the legal authority of what has been done, and must consequently be "approved" at the meeting following the one recorded.

Vacancies are filled by a new election, unless otherwise provided by special rule. In extreme cases, officers may be removed.

The business of special meetings is restricted to that specified in the call.

PART II

MOTIONS

CHAPTER V

THE MAKING, STATING, PUTTING, AND SECONDING OF MOTIONS

"Motion" vs. "Talk;" The Process of Deciding a Matter by Motion and Vote; Words to be Used; When a Motion may be Made; Illustration of the Process; Seconding the Motion; Form for Seconding; Extremes to be Avoided.

30. The "Motion." In the process of the transaction of business there are three stages: 1, the motion; 2, the debate upon the motion; 3, the vote upon the motion. These three are a sort of thread upon which all the procedure, however complicated, is strung. A motion is a proposition that the assembly take some action upon some matter. In order to bring a matter properly before a meeting, it is necessary to make a formal motion. Desultory talk or suggestion followed by general agreement is of no binding value. A motion, regularly made and put to vote, is the basis of business; and only when this is done, can one who is instructed to do a certain thing be held to its performance. This is not saying that a matter may not be informally talked over previous to the making of the motion. But such informal talk is merely preliminary to the regular motion : it does not take its place, and if there is objection, it must be omitted. *The motion alone is the basis of action.*

31. **The Process of Deciding a Matter by Motion and Vote.** In deciding a matter by motion and vote, six steps are essential. These are as follows:—

1. The member rises and addresses the chair.

2. The chairman rises and recognizes the member.

3. The member makes her motion and sits.

4. The chairman states the motion.

5. The chairman gives opportunity for debate, and then asks, Are you ready for the question?

6. The motion is put to vote, and the result declared.

If the motion is seconded, the seconding follows

the third step. This is not included, because it is not *absolutely* essential, while the other steps are.

32. Words to be Used. In making motions, any words may be used which express the speaker's meaning. A motion should be as concise as possible, and should relate to one subject. The motions given in illustration throughout the text of this book are not arbitrary, but are simply indicatory of how a motion should be framed. The speaker should begin by saying, "I move;" not "I motion," or "I move you," but "I move that" (so and so). The chair, in putting the motion before the meeting, should repeat it as nearly as possible as it was made. She may ask for it to be put in writing or may ask the mover to repeat it, in order to have it correct. If it is awkwardly expressed, or is involved, she may, in stating it, put it in better shape by altering the *wording*, but she must not change the *sense* in any way. If she does change the sense, the mover should insist upon repeating it herself, or correcting it.

33. When a Motion may be Made. Any motion may be made at any time when there is no other motion pending. There are also certain technical motions which may be made while others are pending, and these are considered in chapter fourteen. No motion can be made during voting, or while a member has the floor for debate. When a motion is defeated, the matter remains where it was before the motion was made.

34. Illustration of the Process. Let us suppose that a business meeting of the Mendon Women's Club is in progress. The president has called the meeting to order, the records have been read and approved, and, in the "order of business," the item "new business" is reached.

Mrs. Preston wishes to bring before the club a proposition for a public lecture. She rises and says, "Mrs. President," then waits for "recognition;" the chair, rising, "recognizes" her by saying, "Mrs. Preston." Mrs. Preston then "has the floor." She proceeds as follows: "I move that our club hold a public meeting."[1] She then sits, and the president says, "You have heard the motion of Mrs. Preston, that our club hold a public meeting; the matter is before you for discussion." Still standing, the chair waits for, invites, if necessary urges, discussion; and

[1] See Appendix.

when the matter has been debated[1] (during debate
the chair may sit), and it seems to her that all have
spoken who wish, she rises and says, "Are you
ready for the question?" If no one rises to speak,
she then puts the motion to vote as follows: "The
motion is that our club hold a public meeting. All
those who are in favor of the motion will say 'Aye.'
[*Those who favor the project, answer 'Aye.'*] Those
opposed, 'No.' [*Those opposed answer 'No.'*] The
ayes have it" (or "The motion is carried"). If the
"Noes" are in the majority, she declares the result
by saying, "The noes have it" (or, "The motion is
lost"). This declaration of the chair decides the
matter, unless the vote is doubted or reconsidered.
The secretary records the result, and it stands as the
vote of the club, to be in future acted upon. Further motions as to when and where the public meeting shall be held, who shall be the speakers, etc.,
are made and decided by the same forms. In short,
all motions whatsoever follow this same process, with
the exception that, with certain technical motions,
debate is omitted or limited.[2]

---

[1] For rules regarding the limit of debate, see *section* 47.
[2] See Appendix.

35. Seconding the Motion. The practice of
seconding the motion is apt to be regarded as of
too great importance, many persons who do not
even *make* or *put* a motion properly, often insisting
upon the necessity of *seconding* all motions before
they allow them to be discussed.   This is placing
too much value upon a small matter.   The "second"
is merely a sign of approval, and is of the nature of
debate, a person "seconding" when she has nothing
to say, or as a preliminary for her remarks.   Moreover, the practice of certain legislatures [1] and other
large bodies in *not seconding motions* would seem
to indicate that seconding is gradually falling into
disuse, experienced bodies having found that the
omission of the second is useful in saving time and
in subserving that principle of equality by which
every member has an equal right with every other
to introduce a motion and to have it placed before
the assembly.

Therefore, although most of the other authorities

[1] Motions are not seconded in either house of Congress or in the Legisla-
ture of Massachusetts. The same is probably true of most of the other States.
The author has the authority of the Senior Senator from Massachusetts for
saying that "in most bodies of dignity and importance a second to a motion
is not required by parliamentary rule."

in parliamentary law make the seconding obligatory, it is here recommended not to give a too strict adherence to this old method (except in the case of undebatable, irregular, or factious motions), but to leave it optional with the presiding officer, whether or not to require a second, before placing a motion before the meeting.

It is understood, then, that any member *may* second any motion, but *need* not; that the chair *may* ask for a second if none has been given; that the chair *should* place the motion before the meeting without asking for a second, except in certain cases; that the chair may tacitly second any motion herself, if she thinks best, and thus do away with the necessity of asking for a second from the floor. Where seconding is insisted upon, the lack of a second suppresses the motion. A fair-minded chairman will consequently second a proper motion herself rather than allow it to be suppressed.

36. Form for Seconding. When a motion is seconded, the seconding follows the making of the motion. The seconding may be done formally (by rising, addressing the chair, obtaining recognition, and saying, " I second the motion "), or, since it is an unimportant matter, informally, by calling out "second the motion" while seated. The chair then says: "The motion is made and seconded that"—etc. When she seconds it herself, she uses the same words, or says: " It is moved that," etc. When there is no second, she says: "The motion is made," or " Mrs.—— moves," or " It is moved," etc. If she desires to insist upon a second from the floor, she will say: " Is the motion seconded?" In societies where seconding is insisted upon, the members should second at once, and not oblige the chair to ask, thereby saving much time, and preventing the incessant reiteration of the question, "Is the motion seconded?"

37. **Extremes to be Avoided.** There are two extremes which a fair-minded chairman will avoid: *first*, suppressing a motion because it is not seconded; and *second*, hastily putting one to vote without giving a chance for discussion.

As was said in chapter one, nominations for office would better be seconded. The reason for this is that nominations are almost never discussed. Indeed, a good rule to be established in regard to seconding would be this: a second should not ordinarily be insisted upon; but it may be, in the case of nominations, of undebatable motions, and of appeals. In the illustrations in this book, seconding will be omitted. Any society which adopts the *Woman's Manual* as its authority is thereby left free to second motions or not, as it chooses.

SUMMARY

A formal motion, regularly made and put to vote, is the only proper basis for business. Informal talk determines nothing.

There are six essential steps in deciding a matter by motion and vote: addressing the chair, recognition, making the motion, stating the motion, debate, putting the question to vote.

Any words may be used which express the speaker's meaning.

A motion begins with the words, "I move that."

A motion may be made at any time when no other is pending.

Seconding the motion is always permissible, but should not be too strongly insisted upon. The chair may or may not require a second, or she may tacitly second a motion herself.   The chair decides the matter.

A motion should not be suppressed because it is not seconded; neither should one be put to vote hastily without opportunity for debate.

———

CHAPTER VI

THE WITHDRAWAL AND DIVISION OF MOTIONS

Rule for Withdrawal; Withdrawal Illustrated; Exception; Division of Motions; Equivalent Motions.

38. Rule for Withdrawal.   A motion, having been made and stated, is in the possession of the *assembly* and not of the mover, who may "withdraw" it only under certain restrictions.   The rule for withdrawal may be stated as follows: The member who makes a motion may withdraw it, by unanimous consent, before it is put to vote, unless it has been amended or put into a different form from that first moved.   The reason why it cannot

be withdrawn without unanimous consent is because after it has been put before the assembly it
"belongs," so to speak, to the whole body, and
no longer to the mover.   Furthermore, unanimous
consent is the shortest way of· determining the
wish of the meeting; any person could at once
renew the motion if it were allowed to be withdrawn by a majority vote, and time would thereby
be lost.   Even by unanimous consent, it cannot
be withdrawn if it has been amended, for it has
now become involved in other processes which
require their own course of action.   If it has
been seconded, the second must also be withdrawn.
A motion that is withdrawn need not be recorded,
for it is as if it had not been made at all.

39. **Withdrawal Illustrated**.   Matters may
come up in the course of debate which lead the
mover to see that her motion is unnecessary or
undesirable, and she wishes she had not made it.
She may in that case withdraw it.   That is, she
may rise, address the chair, and, being recognized,
may say, "I desire to withdraw my motion." The
chair will then say, "Mrs. —— desires to withdraw
her motion.   Is there any objection?" She waits

for objections, and if there are none, she says,
"The motion is withdrawn." If any one, wishing
it to be further considered, does object to its
withdrawal, that person rises and says, "Mrs.
President, I object." The chair will then say,
"There being objection, the motion cannot be
withdrawn, and is still before you," and the debate
upon it proceeds.

40. Exception. A motion may be withdrawn
before it is stated by the chair, without unanimous
consent, and solely at the will of the mover. Not
having been stated by the chair, it "belongs" to
the mover. This may happen when, after a motion
is made, the chair, or some one through the chair,
knowing of facts or circumstances unknown to the
mover, suggests to her its undesirability or untime-
liness; and she in consequence withdraws it, if
she wishes.

41. Division of Motions. A motion which has
two or more distinct parts may be divided into
as many motions as there are parts, and each one
put to vote separately. This division may be made
by the chair without a vote, if there is no objection; or, a member may move "that the motion

be divided," and this is put to vote like any other motion. For instance, a motion is made "that a committee of three be appointed by the chair to consider the question of holding a public meeting, and be given full powers." This may be divided into four parts, as follows: 1, That a committee be appointed to consider the question of a public meeting; 2, That it consist of three; 3, That it be appointed by the chair; 4, That it be given full powers.

This gives opportunity for debating and amending each proposition separately, and secures a quicker and fairer result than if the whole complex motion were under consideration at once. In precedence, "to divide" ranks with "to amend." *See section 116.*

If the *chair* decides upon the division without a motion, she separates the motion into its obviously distinct parts, putting each to vote. The motion to divide is simply, "I move that the motion be divided," without specifying the manner of division. If this is carried, the chair proceeds to divide the motion, as in the other case.

42. Equivalent Motions. When the negative

of one motion amounts to the affirmative of another and *leaves no alternative*, the decision of one decides the other.　For an example, *see section 50.*

SUMMARY

The mover may withdraw her motion, by unanimous consent, unless it has been amended or modified.

A motion may be withdrawn before it is stated, at the will of the mover.

A motion which has two or more distinct parts may be divided, each part being put to vote separately.

The chair decides upon the manner of division; she may divide without a motion "that the motion be divided," or one may be made to that effect.

A motion which is another's equivalent is decided when that other is decided.

CHAPTER VII

DEBATE

THE RIGHT OF DEBATE; DEBATE DEFINED; WHEN
DEBATE IS IN ORDER; METHOD OF DEBATE
ILLUSTRATED; RULES FOR LIMITING DEBATE;
ILLUSTRATION; THE ARGUMENTS; CONTESTING
THE FLOOR; YIELDING THE FLOOR; COURTESIES
IN DEBATE; GENERAL CONSENT.

43. The Right of Debate. After a motion has
been made, and stated by the chair, it is before the
assembly for consideration. It is now the duty of
the chairman to see that it is fully and fairly considered, and to secure the right of the members
equally to take part in its discussion. On the
other hand, provision is often needed to protect an
assembly from the tendency of members to "talk
against time." To preserve the happy medium
between a tedious or factious debate on the one
hand, and a summary disposal of all debate on the
other, it is well for a society to adopt a few simple
rules to guide and guard its discussions.

44. Debate Defined. Strictly speaking, "debate" means remarks made on opposite sides of a question; it presupposes difference of opinion and conflict of votes. But in its more general sense, it includes all remarks made in relation to a motion, even if all on one side. Debate may therefore be defined as original remarks, spoken, not read from manuscript, by a member of the assembly who has obtained the floor, which remarks should be impersonal[1] and to the point. The speaker may have notes jotted down to aid her; she may recite her speech from memory, or it may be *extempore*, but, as Mr. Crocker says, "debate is not reading a speech."

45. When Debate is in Order. Debate is in order only when a motion is regularly before the meeting. Informal discussion, without a motion to speak to, is not debate. This is allowable (by general consent only), but regular debate is discussion *of a motion.* The motion being made and stated, "debate" follows. Conversely, debate ceases as soon as the motion is put to vote. The chair having asked, "Are you ready for the ques-

[1] See Appendix.

tion?" and no one rising to speak, the motion passes from the debatable stage, and is put to vote, when debate cannot be resumed. By general consent, in voting by *vivâ voce*, by rising, and by show of hands, debate may be resumed after the affirmative is put. In case it is resumed, the vote, when finally taken, is taken again *on both sides*. If both sides have been taken, *debate* cannot be resumed in any case, and any talk or discussion that may follow the declaration of a vote is of no value; the matter is decided. If there are special rules, these govern the debate; and if the previous question has been ordered, there can be no more debate, even by unanimous consent.

46. Method of Debate Illustrated. Let us suppose that at a meeting of the Mendon Women's Club, a motion "that a public meeting be held" has been made and placed before the meeting. Debate is now in order, and the chair invites discussion, saying: "The motion is now before you for discussion, and the chair hopes the members will all express their views freely." Mrs. Paine rises, "addresses the chair," is "recognized," and thus "has the floor." She proceeds to speak in

favor of the public meeting, speaking strictly upon
that subject alone, and giving such reasons as ap-
pear to her to be good. She avoids saying "It
seems to me " if possible, guards against repetition
and prolixity, and is careful not to indulge in any
anti-climax. If an inexperienced speaker, she
should be encouraged by the chair to go on, even if
she does not express herself so well as might be —
the *way* of speaking being secondary to the *speaking*.
If she is wise, she will not apologize for her words,
either in beginning or closing, but let them stand
for what they are. If she has occasion during her
speech to allude to any other member, she will not
do so by name, but will say instead, " the member
on my right," or " our secretary," or " another
speaker," or " one of my opponents," or any impersonal term which shall indicate the one meant.
Directly addressing one another by name is unpar-
liamentary. Having said all she has to say, she
stops and sits down.

   If no one rises immediately to continue the discussion, the chair will invite others, saying, " There
must be others who have some opinion in this matter. Do not wait for one another, friends ; this

question should be fully discussed." It is not well
for the chair to call upon members by name, except in rare cases, as when some particular person
is specially well-informed on a subject; for, where
this practice is followed, those who are not called
upon never dare to speak, and those who are,
wait for an invitation; the consequence being that
the freedom and spontaneity of debate, which make
its chief value, are prevented. It is better for the
chair to wait, in the midst of an oppressive silence
(hard though this is), for the spirit to move, than
to attempt to coerce debate by indicating who shall
speak. After a time (which will grow shorter as
the members gain courage by practice) some other
member rises and gives her reasons, as well as she
can, for or against the project. Others follow,
until all have spoken who wish. No one having
the floor, or rising to speak, the chair then says,
"Are you ready for the question?" and, no one
rising to speak, she puts the motion to vote.

47. **Rules for Limiting Debate.** In the illustration given above, it is assumed that there are no
rules limiting debate, but that all speak when and
as long as they wish; and this is the best and gen-

eral practice when the discussion relates solely to
business to be done, and also in societies where it
is difficult to persuade members to speak at all on
any subject.   A judicious and kindly president will
draw out all the discussion possible from those
present who can overcome their natural timidity,
and rules *limiting* debate will be undesirable.

But, in societies where the object is to learn to
debate, especially when the members are experienced, or on special occasions where there is a
limited time and general interest upon some desig-
nated topic, it is well to guard against the monopoly
of debate by one or two persons, by adopting certain rules, either for temporary or for permanent
use.   These rules will restrict the speakers as to
the time and as to the order of their speaking.
The simple rules for an ordinary debate are the
following : —

*No one shall speak more than once until all have
spoken who wish.*

*No one shall speak longer than five minutes at one
time.*

*The leaders shall each have ten minutes to open the
debate and five minutes to close.*

The prescribed time may be longer or shorter of course, and it is not necessary that the leaders close ; it will be found not desirable to have them, when the time is limited.

These few rules are all that will be necessary in ordinary cases. The chair must enforce them by rising, rapping, and adding, if necessary, " The speaker's time has expired." Or, a bell may be rung. One who persists in going on is disorderly. If one has already spoken, the chair will say: "Are there others who wish to speak?"

The practice of extending a speaker's time is correct, but, as it defeats the purpose of the rules, the extension should not often be made. If it be desired to extend the time, some one obtains the floor, and makes a motion "that the speaker's time be extended —— minutes," and if this is carried, she goes on. It may be said in general, upon this point, that, having rules, it is better to adhere to them, except in extreme cases. It might be well to adopt this additional rule : —

Only by a unanimous vote shall a speaker's time be extended.

48. Illustration. The Mendon Women's Club.

having progressed so far as to discuss papers informally, decides to go a step farther, and to have
a formal debate. A resolution is prepared, in
proper form, by a member or members appointed
to do it, on some subject of interest, such as the
tariff-law, the single-tax theory, or a local topic.
This resolution should be affirmative and not negative; that is, it should read, "*Resolved*, that the
present tariff *is* of benefit;" and not, "*is not* of
benefit." This is to prevent confusion in the
minds of the debaters and hearers as to which
side they are considering. Two or four members
are then selected, either by nomination from the
floor, or by appointment of the chair (as is voted),
to be the leaders in the debate. It is best to
appoint them one by one, in the following order;
and care should be taken that each understands
which side she is on: First affirmative, first negative, second affirmative, second negative. It is
then voted to guide the debate by the rules given
in the preceding section.

When the time arrives, the chair says, "The programme for this afternoon is a debate upon the
following subject: '*Resolved*, that the present

tariff-law is of benefit to the business interests of our country.' Mrs. Paine, being first upon the affirmative, will open the debate." Mrs. Paine rises, addresses the chair, is recognized, and proceeds with her remarks until the chair indicates to her that her time is up. The chair then says, "Mrs. Robbins, the first on the negative, will continue the debate," and Mrs. Robbins follows Mrs. Paine's example. She is followed by Mrs Preston as "second on the affirmative," and she, in her turn, by Mrs. Burns, as "second on the negative." The leaders having finished, the chair says, "The debate is now open to all present, each being allowed not more than five minutes;" and all then speak who wish. If the leaders are to close, time is taken for that purpose from the other speakers. If not, the debate is over when all have spoken who wish, or when the time has come for adjournment, or when the previous question is ordered. Debate having closed, the chair puts the resolution to vote, as follows: "Those in favor of the resolution, 'That the present tariff-law is of benefit to the business interests of the country,' will rise and stand until counted. [*The affirmatives*

rise, the secretary counts them and notes the result.]
Those opposed to the resolution will rise and stand
until counted. [*The negatives rise and are counted.*
Then the president, to whom the secretary hands
the result, goes on:] Twenty-five have voted in
the affirmative, and thirty in the negative, and the
resolution is lost."

49. The Arguments. Sometimes a vote is
taken upon the merits of the *arguments*, as well
as, or instead of, the merits of the *question*, the
members voting upon the side which they consider
to have been best presented, whether or not they
concur in the views expressed. This is not spe
cially commendable, since it tends to encourage
oratory rather than sincerity.

It should be the aim of all debaters to inform
themselves as thoroughly as possible; to be truth-
ful, correct, and concise; and at the same time to
press the merits of their own side emphatically,
and to use any fair means to show the fallacy,
inexpediency, or injustice, of the opposing side.

50. Contesting the Floor. As already stated,
the member who is recognized by the chair, "has
the floor;" and she is entitled to speak, without

interruption, for her allotted time, provided she speaks in order. It may happen, however, that two persons rise and address the chair at the same moment. In this case, unless one of them yields [saying, "I yield to Miss ——, Mrs. President"] and seats herself, the chair decides between the two. This she does by calling the name of the one she first saw or heard. If she is in doubt, she will recognize the one farthest from her, or the one who has not spoken, or who speaks seldom, rather than the other; if one has risen and addressed the chair, and the other has risen only, or spoken only, the one properly proceeding has the preference.

If the one not recognized believes that *she* is entitled to the floor, she may insist, remaining standing, and saying: "Mrs. President, I believe I addressed the chair first," or words to that effect. The chair then says: "Does Mrs. —— (the one recognized) yield to Mrs. ——?" and if she does not, she puts the question to vote, saying: "The question is: which of these members was first up? Those in favor of giving the floor to" [mentioning the one she has recognized] "will say 'Aye.'" If the ayes prevail, the other person sits down; if the noes prevail, she has the floor, and the one recognized sits down. It is not necessary to take the vote upon the other name, since the decision of the vote upon one name necessarily decides that upon the other, leaving no alternative. This is an example of "equivalent motions."

If there are more than two contestants, however, as many votes must be taken as are necessary to come to a decision. Such action is called "contesting the floor," and it rarely occurs except in legislatures. The members of ordinary societies will generally acquiesce in the chair's decision, or amicably yield one to another. But this provision is useful in case of unfairness on the part of the chair, or urgency on the part of the speaker's cause.

51. Yielding the Floor. It often happens, during an interesting debate, that some member will wish to interrupt another, to "ask a question," either in good faith or, as often happens, to point out a fallacy. In this case, the member speaking may or may not allow the question to be interjected. If she does "yield the floor" for that purpose, *she loses the floor*, in case the one interrupting shall choose to continue her remarks further, and can only resume it provided she again succeeds in obtaining it in the regular way. For example: Mrs. Paine is speaking concerning the public meeting of the woman's club, and Mrs. Granger wishes to ask her a question. She rises and says, "Mrs. President, will the speaker allow a question?" The chair rises and says, "Will Mrs. Paine yield the floor for a question?" Mrs. Paine may say, "Certainly," remain standing, listen to the question, reply to it or not, and go on after Mrs. Granger has seated herself. Or, not wishing to have her train of argument interrupted, Mrs. Paine may say, "After I have finished, Mrs. President, I shall be glad to answer any question, if I am able," and proceed with her remarks, Mrs. Granger sitting down. If she allows the question, she runs the risk of losing the floor, and also the trend of her thoughts; in deciding the matter, she will be guided by her knowledge of Mrs. Granger's views, which, if unfavorable to her own, would better not be allowed at that time.

In asking her question, Mrs. Granger would use this form: " I would like to ask the speaker, through you, Mrs. President, whether" etc. She may then go on to answer it herself, and to make an argument, in spite of the fact that Mrs. Paine is still standing. Finally, if Mrs. Granger goes on until Mrs. Paine sits down, Mrs. Paine has "lost the floor," and if she wishes to resume, she can only do so in the regular way, or by "general consent." This is a sharp practice, it is true, but since it is parliamentary, it may well be guarded against. Interruptions are disturbing, both to the speaker and the hearers, and should be discouraged. Warrington says : —

"An experienced debater will seldom lose anything by interruption; an inexperienced one ought not to be subjected to loss or discomfiture by any such event."

When the floor, instead of being voluntarily yielded, is taken from a member by a question of privilege or of order, it is not thereby lost, but still belongs to that member, who has the first right to it after the prior question is settled. The rule is that if one *voluntarily* yields, she loses the right to the floor, while if she yields of necessity, she retains that right. *See sections 149 and 153.*

52. Courtesies in Debate. While courtesy is always to be regarded, it is not to be carried so far as to endanger one's cause. It is not discourtesy to refuse to yield the floor, provided one declines in a courteous manner. Neither is it discourteous to hold the floor, having gained it, provided it is gained fairly.

A custom has grown up in Congress of allowing certain members precedence over other members in debate. The chairman of a committee, or the originator of a measure, for instance, is given opportunity and time to the exclusion of the general membership. This may be necessary in Congress, but any tendency toward such "courtesies" (as they are called) in ordinary societies, should be discountenanced. To give special privileges to any member over any other is to endanger that freedom which is the soul of debate as well as its safety.

53. "General Consent." A number of procedures, otherwise irregular, may be admitted by "general consent," and "general consent" means *unanimous* consent. Routine business is carried on, debate is allowed when really out of order, and similar informalities, (instances of which will be cited here and there in this book,) are allowed. In any of these cases, *if one person objects*, the presiding officer must proceed regularly. Business may frequently be facilitated in this way, but the practice must be carefully guarded against misuse. There are also certain procedures which *require* unanimous consent, such as the withdrawal of a motion, and expunging from the record. In such cases, the unanimous consent must be ascertained and not assumed. The chair will proceed as in *section 39*, or still better, will say: "this matter requires unanimous consent. Those in favor," etc., and if there is one dissenting voice, it is lost.

SUMMARY

Debate consists of spoken remarks, made by one who has properly obtained the floor. They should be impersonal and to the point.

After a motion is placed before the meeting, debate is in order. Any remarks that precede the making or follow the putting to vote of a motion are not debate, and have no influence upon action.

By unanimous consent, debate may be re-opened after the affirmative vote is taken.

Members should address the chair in opening, wait for recognition, speak to the motion, and sit down when they have finished.

The chair should not invite members to speak by calling upon them by name.

In small assemblies, debate is most successful when unrestricted by any rules, each one speaking when and as long as she wishes.

When the time is limited, or when leaders are appointed for a formal debate, rules restricting to a certain time, and prescribing the order of speaking, are needful.

A speaker's time may be extended, but it is better to adhere to the rules.

It is better to take the vote upon the merits of the question, rather than upon the merits of the arguments.

The member recognized is entitled to the floor, but another, who thinks herself entitled to it, may claim it, and the matter is decided by vote.

A member who *yields* the floor loses the right to it. It is not discourteous to refuse to yield.

When the floor is *taken* from a speaker, she does

not lose the right to it, but resumes it when the matter which interrupted her is settled.

Special privileges, given to certain members over others, endanger the freedom of debate.

"General consent" means unanimous consent. By general consent, certain irregularities may be admitted.

CHAPTER VIII

THE PREVIOUS QUESTION, OR THE CLOSING OF DEBATE

PREVIOUS QUESTION DEFINED; USE OF THE PRE-
VIOUS QUESTION; ITS EFFECT; DEBATE UPON
IT; ILLUSTRATION; PREVIOUS QUESTION *vs.*
MAIN QUESTION; ITS EFFECT UPON OTHER
MOTIONS; ITS EFFECT UPON A PART OF THE
MAIN QUESTION; "QUESTION! QUESTION!"
CLOSING DEBATE AT A STATED TIME.

54. Previous Question Defined. The term "previous question" is a technicality that has come down to us from the English Parliament, but the use of which is very different here. With us, the motion for the previous question is a motion "that the vote upon the main question be taken at once, without further debate." It is therefore equivalent to a motion "to close debate," and the two motions: "I move the previous question," and "I move that debate be now closed," are synonymous. Mr. Fish and Mr. Crocker recommend the simple form "that debate be now closed." But at present the form "previous question" is in general use. Societies may use either form they choose.

55. The Use of the Previous Question. It is not universally agreed that a motion to close debate should be allowed as a part of the regular procedure, — the question whether debate ought ever to be closed, until all who wish have spoken, being a moot one. In large assemblies, this motion would seem to be necessary, in order to prevent interminable debates, and it can always be voted down by the majority. In smaller assemblies, it may well be used sparingly, and should be prohibited by rule wherever there is danger of its *constant* use in choking discussion or preventing the expression of the views of the minority. When it is not prohibited by special rule, it is parliamentary to employ it. It might be well for societies to make a rule that it shall require a two-thirds vote.[1] This would guard against the choking of debate by the vote of a bare majority. The motion to close debate, in either of its forms, is not allowed in the Senate of the United States, or in the State Senates of Massachusetts and New York; it is used in the other branch of these bodies. Any society which does not favor its use may make a special rule to the effect that "the motion for the previous question shall be prohibited in our club."

56. **Its Effect.** It has been already stated that when there are no rules limiting debate, debate is unrestricted; it continues till all have spoken who wish, or until time for adjournment, when the chair, after asking, " Are you ready for the question? " puts the motion to vote. Debate thus ceases of its own accord, so to speak. When it is desired to terminate debate and come to a decision, the call for the previous question is the method employed. The effect of this call is to close debate immedi-

[1] See Appendix.

ately upon the subject before the meeting. That is, the mere making and stating of the motion for the previous question, *before it is decided*, closes the debate upon the main question. If, when put to vote,[1] the motion for the previous question is defeated, the debate upon the subject is resumed. If the motion prevails, debate upon the main question is closed, and it is at once put to vote. The points to be remembered in regard to this motion are, *first*, that it is simply a motion to close debate and nothing more; and, *second*, that when it is moved, there come before the meeting for immediate vote, two motions, the independent motion (the main question under discussion), and the dependent motion (to close debate). A vote is to be taken upon both these motions; first, upon the previous question, and then, if this prevails, upon the main question, debate on the latter being meanwhile suspended. Of necessity, the previous question applies only to debatable motions, and it would seem proper to assume, as a general rule, that any debatable motion is open to the call for the previous question.

---

[1] The form for putting the question is: " Shall the main question be now put?" This means: Shall further debate be omitted and a vote taken at once?

57. Debate of the Motion for the Previous Question.[1] The motion to close debate may itself be debated for a limited time, usually fixed at ten minutes at most; or, it may be decided *by rule* to be undebatable. There is nothing to be said, except to give some reason why the main question should not then be voted upon, and this can be said very quickly. If a speaker, in debating this motion, branches off into a discussion of the main question, she is out of order, and the chair will stop her. This motion is not used in committees.

58. Illustration of the Previous Question. The Mendon Women's Club is debating the question of holding a public meeting. Miss Lovell thinks it has been debated long enough, and wishes it to come to a vote. Mrs. Paine having finished her remarks and taken her seat, Miss Lovell rises, obtains the floor in the usual way, and says: "I move the previous question." The chair says: "The previous question is moved. Shall the main question be now put?" If there is no debate (of the motion for the previous question), she goes on at once, saying: "Those in favor * * *" If there

---

[1] See Appendix.

is debate, this is limited, and is strictly confined to giving reasons why the main question should or should not then be voted upon. When the ten minutes are up (or before, if debate ceases), the chair says: "The limit of debate having expired, the vote will now be taken. Those in favor of the motion for the previous question will say 'Aye,' * * those opposed, 'No.' * * It is carried, and the previous question is ordered." She then goes on without pause, and puts to vote the main question, saying: "Those in favor of the motion that the club hold a public meeting will say 'Aye' * * *" The matter is thus ended. If any one attempts to debate after the previous question is ordered, she is ruled out of order. The club having voted to come to a vote upon the main question, nothing may interpose to prevent the taking of such vote.

If the motion is lost, instead of carried, the chair will say: "The noes have it; the motion for the previous question being lost, debate will continue." The discussion is then resumed, to go on until the previous question is moved again (which may be done any time), or until it closes by mutual consent, or by adjournment, or by some other motion which disposes temporarily of the main question.

If the other form of the motion is used, Miss Lovell will say, instead: "I move that the debate do now close." The chair will state it in the same form, saying: "It is moved that the debate do now close. Are you ready? Those in favor * * * It is carried, and the debate is closed." She then proceeds as above. This latter form is simpler, but not in such general use, as yet. If the form "previous question" is used, it will be well, in societies unfamiliar with its meaning, for the chair to explain its effect. She may say: "The previous question is moved. The effect of this motion is to suspend debate until it is voted that debate shall, or shall not now close; if it prevails, all debate upon the main question closes, and an immediate vote upon it follows. Shall the main question be now put?" and so on, as above.

59. "Previous Question" *vs.* Main Question. The word "previous" is a little confusing, and care should be taken that the members understand that when they are voting upon the motion for the previous question, they are not voting upon the

main question itself, but simply upon the motion to *close debate* upon the main question. *Two* votes are taken, the vote upon the previous question, and then, in case the vote for the previous question prevails, the vote upon the main question, with any attachments which may be pending, the two votes following each other, with no business intervening.

60. **Effect of the Previous Question upon Other Motions.** After the previous question is moved and stated, the following action can be taken : the raising of a question of privilege, or of a question of order, *provided it strictly relates to the subject* (namely, the call for the previous question); a motion to adjourn, to take a recess, or to fix the time for reassembling, a motion to lay upon the table, and also, in brief, any motion relating to the *verbal* perfecting of the main question, or to the manner of taking the vote upon it. After the previous question is ordered, nothing can intervene to prevent an immediate vote on the main question, except the question of "no quorum," or a motion as to the manner of voting. Everything must be decided without debate.

If the motion to close debate is carried while a motion "to postpone," or a motion "to commit" is pending, each of these is "cut off" or negatived, thereby. The reason for this is that when the assembly votes to close debate, it is a sign that they wish to come to an immediate vote, and an immediate vote would be invalidated by postponement or commitment. Pending amendments are not cut off, because they tend to perfect the main question, but debate upon them is closed, and no new ones can be admitted. The previous question, therefore, cuts off debate upon everything, and also cuts off the existence itself of the two motions to commit and to postpone. Its effect upon reconsideration is considered in *sections 77 and 82.*

61. **Its Effect when Moved upon a Part of the Main Question.** There is a conflict of authorities as to whether the previous question can be moved upon *a part* of the main question, one opinion being that whenever moved, it closes debate upon the *whole* subject, and that therefore it cannot be moved upon a part of it. In reply, it might be said (in general) that, of necessity, the only motions upon which the previous question can

be moved are debatable ones, and since the only important debatable motions that are a part of other motions are those to postpone, to commit, to amend, and to postpone indefinitely, it is chiefly in regard to those that the doubt arises. Can one move the previous question upon an amendment, or upon a motion to commit, to postpone, or to postpone indefinitely, and have it apply simply to that? That is, can a member say: "I move the previous question upon the motion to commit," for instance, and not have that motion apply to the main question also?

There seems to be no good reason why debate cannot be closed upon a motion to commit or to postpone, or (especially) upon a much-debated amendment, distinct from the main question. There is certainly necessity for it, if the motion is long discussed; and there is no hardship attendant upon it. For these reasons, the following practice is recommended: the previous question may be moved upon the motions to postpone, to commit, and to postpone indefinitely, and upon an amendment or its secondary; also upon appeals. If, after it is moved on the part, it is also moved upon the main question, — the two motions being pending at once, — the motion to close debate on the main question is put first.   If a motion to close debate on the main question were made *first*, one to close debate on a part could not then be made.

When the motion to close debate on a part of a question is made, it must be definitely so stated. It will then be, "I move the previous question upon the amendment," etc., instead of simply, "I move the previous question."   If made and carried, the *part* affected is put to vote at once, and then debate goes on upon the rest of the subject.

62. "Question! Question!"   The calling out of "question" from members while seated, is not equivalent to the motion for the previous question.   Like the calls "By the chair," and "From the floor," in nominating officers, it need not be heeded by the chair.   See footnote to page 14. The chair may, however, by general consent, consider such a call as an indication that the assembly is ready to vote, and say: "Are you ready for the question?" and then put it to vote. But she is not obliged to do so, and may allow

debate to continue in spite of it. One who wishes to have the debate close would better properly obtain the floor, and make the regular motion for the previous question.

63. Closing Debate at a Stated Time. Besides the motion for the previous question (which is a motion to close debate at once), there is the motion to close debate at some stated future time. This is the same as any other motion, except that it may be made when another is pending. It is better to make it, if possible, before the debate begins, but it may be made during the debate. Its use is to prevent an undue, and at the same time to secure a sufficient, debate. The form of this motion is as follows: "I move that debate upon this motion shall close at four o'clock." This is debated for a limited time, amended as to the hour perhaps, and put to vote. If carried, when the time comes, debate ceases, and the subject is voted upon. If more debate is desired by the majority, it may be reconsidered, in common with most other motions, and debate be continued.

Those who wish to study the previous question further are recommended to read Cushing's manual, paragraphs 63–66 and 170; Warrington's manual, sections 53–60; Crocker's Parliamentary Procedure, sections 55–58; Fish's Guide, pp. 87–90; and Reed's Rules, sections 123–128.

SUMMARY

The motion "for the previous question" and the motion "to close debate" are synonymous.

The previous question is moved when it is desired by the mover to close debate at once upon the subject before the meeting.

When it is not prohibited by special rule, it is parliamentary to use the previous question in order to shut off debate.

The effect of the motion for the previous question is to suspend debate upon the main question until the vote upon the previous question is taken.

If the motion for the previous question prevails, the main question is brought to an immediate vote, without further debate.

If it is lost, debate upon the main question is resumed.

As a general rule, motions that are debatable may have the previous question moved upon them.

The moving of the previous question cuts off debate upon the main question, but may itself be debated for a limited time.

When the motion to close debate is made, two motions are brought before the meeting: one upon the previous question (or motion to close debate), and one upon the main question (or subject under discussion).

After the previous question is called for, and before it is put to vote, any of the few motions that may supervene must be decided without debate. New amendments are cut off, also pending motions to postpone and to commit. Motions regarding adjournment, the motion to table, questions of privilege and of order, and motions regarding the verbal perfecting of the measure and the manner of voting, are admissible.

If the previous question is moved upon an amendment or upon any debatable dependent motion, the vote is taken upon the dependent question and not upon the main question. The mover of such a motion must distinctly state *upon what* she wishes debate to close. The simple motion "for the previous question" closes debate upon, and brings to a vote the *main question* itself.

The calling of "Question, question" is not the motion for the previous question, and need have no effect in closing debate or compelling a vote.

A motion to close debate at some stated future time is a useful means for limiting debate within fair limits. It is better to make it before the debating begins.

CHAPTER IX

VOTING

FORM FOR PUTTING A MOTION TO VOTE; RAISING OF HANDS AND RISING; "THE USUAL MANNER;" BOTH SIDES TO BE PUT; DOUBTING THE VOTE; TIES; THE CHAIR'S PREROGATIVE IN CASE OF TIES; RIGHT OF THE CHAIR TO VOTE AT ALL TIMES; THE ROLL–CALL; VOTING BY BALLOT; DECISION BY LESS OR MORE THAN A MAJORITY.

64. Form for Putting a Motion to Vote. The formula for voting has already been given in chapter five, it being inseparable from the motion itself; but it may well be repeated. After discussion has closed, the chair, rising, repeats the motion, and puts it to vote as follows: "The motion is that our club hold a public meeting. All those in favor will say 'Aye' [*the ayes respond*]; those opposed, 'No' [*the noes respond*]. It is a vote." Or, "The ayes have it," or "the motion is carried." If the noes are in the majority, she will say: "The noes have it," or "the motion is lost." This last utterance of the chair is called "declaring the vote," and this "declaration" decides the matter. This method is called the *vivâ voce* vote, or "acclamation."

If no one responds at all, on either side, by general consent the motion is presumed to be carried, the supposition being that all who do not take the trouble to oppose are in favor. It is better to insist upon an expression in such a case, and to take another vote, the chair having the power to order the ayes and noes to be taken again.[1]

65. Raising of Hands and Rising. A vote may also be taken by a raising of the right hand or by standing. The *vivâ voce* vote is shortest and simplest, and therefore the best for ordinary occasions. When a *count* is desirable, one of these

[1] See Appendix.

other methods is employed.   The chair will then
say: "Those in favor will raise the right hand," or,
"rise and stand until counted."   The affirmatives
will then respond in the manner indicated; the
secretary (or two "tellers" appointed by the chair)
will count them, and give the result to the chair.
The negative side will then be put in the same
way, the chair finally declaring the vote as follows: "Fifteen have voted in the affirmative, and
twenty-five in the negative.   The motion is lost."
Only those who vote are counted.

66. "**The Usual Manner.**"   Whichever of
these methods of voting is used, it is the place
of the chair to indicate it, in asking for the vote.
That is, she will say: "Those in favor will say
'Aye'" (or "will rise," etc.) and *not* say: "All
those in favor will manifest it in the usual manner."   There is no "usual manner," and when
this phrase is used, an assembly will not know
definitely what to do.   Some say "Aye" (that
being their "usual manner"), while others raise
the hand (that being their "usual manner"), and
uncertainty ensues.   Even in a permanent society,
where the members attend regularly and have one

way of responding, it is better for the president to indicate the manner for each vote to be taken; and in a temporary or a mixed assembly, it is absolutely necessary so to do.

67. Both Sides to be Put. The vote is not decided until *both sides* have been put and the chair has declared the result. If only the affirmative is put, or if, both sides having been put, the vote is not declared, it is not properly finished, nor legally binding. An inexperienced chairman is quite apt to forget this, and to put the vote thus: "Those in favor will say 'Aye;' it is a vote;" or again: "Those in favor will say 'Aye;' those opposed, 'No;'" leaving out the declaration. The motion is correctly put when the following order is observed: 1, The chair asks for the affirmative vote; 2, The affirmatives respond; 3, The chair asks for the negative vote; 4, The negatives respond; 5, The chair declares the result.

68. Doubting the Vote. When those in favor and those opposed are nearly or quite equal in number, there is apt to be a doubt as to the result of a *viva voce* vote. After both sides have responded, if the chair cannot tell which is in the majority, she says: "The chair is in doubt. Will those in favor of the motion rise and stand until counted?" The proceedings then follow the course described in *section 65.*

Furthermore, in case a member does not agree with the chair's declaration, that member may "doubt the vote." *Illustration:* a motion having been put to vote, and the chair (believing that there are more ayes than noes) having declared "It is a vote," Mrs. Robbins, who thinks there are, or may be, more noes than ayes, rises, and, without waiting for recognition, says: "Mrs. President, I doubt the vote." She then sits, and the chair says: "The vote is doubted; those in favor will rise and stand until counted," and so on, as in *section 65.*

Instead of asking the members to stand, the president may ask for a show of hands, but the rising vote is less liable to mistake. In a very large audience, the voters may be asked to divide into two parties, one going to the right, and the other to the left side of the hall. It is obvious that this clumsy method is not desirable except in extreme cases, and in temporary meetings. In large, permanent organizations, with a list of members, when a vote is doubted, the roll-call, or what is called in legislatures, "the yeas and nays," is the proper method to employ, unless the simple rising vote prove sufficient.

If a *vivâ voce* vote is not doubted, it stands as declared by the chair, even if it be afterward ascertained to be wrong, the supposition being that, if they do not at once doubt it, the members acquiesce in the chair's decision.

69. **Ties.** When those who have voted in the affirmative and those who have voted in the negative are exactly equal in number, there is said to be "a tie." In this case, one side exactly neutralizes the other, and the motion is therefore defeated. The reason why a tie defeats is because a majority is necessary to carry a motion, and a tie is one less than a majority. It defeats simply because it does not carry. *See section 155* for an exception.[1]

70. **The Chair's Prerogative.** When there is a tie vote, it becomes the prerogative of the pre-

---

[1] Voting by proxy is never permissible except when specially authorized by the rules of the society in question.

siding officer (if she has not voted already) to vote, and thus determine the result. This she is not obliged to do, however, and if she does not, the tie remains and the measure is lost. If she is in favor of the motion, she will, in declaring the vote, announce as follows: "Twenty have voted in the affirmative, and twenty in the negative; the chair is to be counted in the affirmative, and the motion is carried." If she is opposed, she will say: "Twenty have voted in the affirmative, and twenty in the negative. The measure is lost." Or, she may say: "The chair is to be counted in the negative, and the measure is lost," using her own option as to whether she will vote and make a majority, or allow the motion to fail by a tie alone, the result being the same in either case. The only advantage in the latter method is that she shows the courage of her convictions.

The chair may also *vote to make a tie*, and thus defeat a motion. If twenty have voted in favor, and nineteen against, and the chair wishes to defeat the motion, she will say, in declaring the vote: "Twenty have voted in the affirmative and nineteen in the negative; the chair votes with the negative, and the motion is lost."

71. **Right of the Chair to Vote.** The president, being a member of the assembly, has the same right to express her choice and to be counted as has every other member. This right is seldom exercised except in case of a tie, but it exists, the only exception being when the presiding officer is not a member, as in the case of the Vice-President of the United States, who, as President of the Senate, has no vote unless the Senate be equally divided. The President *pro tempore* of the U. S. Senate is a member, and entitled to vote.

Where the roll-call is used, the presiding officer's name is called in turn, with those of the other members, and she responds or not. If she does respond, and the vote is a tie, she cannot vote again, for no one is entitled to two votes. If she does not respond, and there is a tie, she will, in declaring the vote, declare her own vote in the manner already shown.

72. **The Roll-Call.** The *vivâ voce* and the rising vote, the show of hands and the division into two groups, have already been explained.

The roll-call, unlike these others, is not employed at the option of the chair, but by a motion and vote. In cases where it is desirable to secure a record of votes in order to know where persons stand upon a certain measure, the yeas and nays are useful and necessary. And since it might be difficult to secure a majority vote in favor of having the roll called, it is usually provided by rule that a small proportion of the members present (say one-fifth) shall have a right to demand it. This provision is almost universal in deliberative bodies, and is recommended for all permanent societies.

When the time comes for the vote to be taken, or at any time previous, any member who wishes a record of votes, obtains the floor in the usual way, and moves: "That when the vote is taken, it be taken by yeas and nays." This motion is put to vote without debate, and if one-fifth of those present vote in the affirmative, the chair declares: "One-fifth having voted in the affirmative, the yeas and nays are ordered." The secretary, or clerk, then rises, takes the alphabetical list, and calls off each name, slowly and clearly, speaking it a second time (but not a third) if the person does not respond at first. Each member, as her name is called, answers " *Yes* "[1] or "*No*" (not "Yea" and "Nay"), the clerk marking each name with a cross or other symbol, and indicating in some way which are yeas and which nays. A good way is to mark the yeas on the right of the name, and the nays on the left, and then they will be all ready to count in columns. The votes are then counted by the secretary,[2] and the result announced in the same way as in declaring the rising vote. This is called "taking the yeas and nays," not "the ayes and noes."

73. Voting by Ballot. When secrecy is desired, a vote is taken by ballot. This method has already been explained in *section* 14. It is a slow process, desirable chiefly in elections (of members, officers, delegates, committees, etc.), and upon questions where members are prevented, for personal reasons, from debating and voting openly. A motion for a ballot is made and put to vote like any ordinary motion, and is decided by the majority.

[1] In distinction from *vivâ voce* voting, where the response is "Aye."

[2] An experienced clerk will sometimes count as she goes along, marking 1, 2, 3, 4, against the names on each side, as they respond.

74. Deciding by Less or More than a Majority.

It is the general rule that a majority, for or against, decides a vote; and this is true in all except a few cases. Only one-fifth of those present is required for the calling of the yeas and nays; in amending a constitution, and in expulsion of members, a two-thirds vote, and in suspension of rules a unanimous vote, should be required. Any other matter, the carrying of which by a bare majority would work hardship, should be protected by a rule requiring a larger vote. A two-thirds vote means two-thirds of those *voting*.

SUMMARY

The three ordinary ways of voting are by responding "Aye" and "No" (called a *vivâ voce* vote), by raising the right hand, and by rising. If no one responds on either side, the motion is presumed to be carried.

Whichever method is employed, the chair should indicate it in putting the motion to vote. She should not say: "Manifest it in the usual manner."

In putting to vote, both the affirmative and the negative sides must be put, and the result must be declared by the chair.

Any *vivâ voce* vote may be doubted, either by the chair or by a member. When doubted, the sense of the meeting is taken again by a rising vote, or by some other method which secures a count.

A tie vote is one in which both sides are equal in number. A tie defeats the motion.

In case of a tie, the chair may vote in the affirmative, thus *carrying* the motion; or she may vote in the negative, or not vote at all, thus refusing to break the tie, and *defeating* the motion. She may also vote so as to make a tie.

The chairman, when a member, may always vote, but usually will not, except in case of a tie.

If one-fifth of those present desire it, a vote may be taken by the roll-call of members. They then respond "Yes" or "No."

Where secrecy is desired, voting by written or printed ballot is employed.

Motions are usually decided by the majority. More or less than a majority may decide certain questions, and each society will adopt its own special rules on these matters.

Motions relating to the manner of taking the vote are undebatable, and not amendable.

CHAPTER X

RECONSIDERATION OF VOTES

RECONSIDERATION DEFINED; NATURE OF THE MOTION TO RECONSIDER; ITS EFFECT; TECHNICAL RECONSIDERATION; WHEN THE MOTION TO RECONSIDER IS MADE; WHO MAY MAKE IT; A POSSIBLE COMPROMISE OF CONFLICTING OPINIONS; DEBATE UPON RECONSIDERATION; THE " PREVAILING SIDE; " ILLUSTRATION; VOTES THAT CANNOT BE RECONSIDERED; THIS MOTION TO BE SPARINGLY EMPLOYED.

75. **Reconsideration Defined.**   After the vote has been taken upon a motion, and that motion is carried, or lost, the general rule is that the matter is ended. It is supposable, however, that members may change their minds, and wish to change their

votes, and, in order to provide for this, parliamentary practice admits of what is called "the motion to reconsider." As its name implies, this is a motion to *consider again*, and its legitimate use is to prevent or reverse hasty or ill-considered action.

76. Nature of the Motion to Reconsider. The motion to reconsider is a motion to reconsider *a vote*, and not to reconsider *a motion*. It is applied to a question after the vote upon it has been taken, and its object is to "reconsider," or take again, such vote.

77. Its Effect. The effect of this motion, *if it prevails*, is to place again before the meeting the subject (the vote upon which has been reconsidered), in precisely the same condition as if the vote had never been passed. It cancels the vote, and re-opens the topic for discussion. Debate is resumed (this is true whether the previous question had been moved upon the vote or not), the question is re-opened for any and all action, and is finally voted on again.

The effect of this motion, *if it is lost*, is to deny the re-opening of the subject, and to clinch or re-affirm the vote upon it; in short, it *closes the matter*,

finally, and for good ; for it is a parliamentary principle that *no vote can be twice reconsidered.* This
means that only one motion to reconsider can be
made in reference to any one vote. Whether the
motion prevails or not, it cannot be repeated; having been once reconsidered, the vote stands. A
measure thus twice considered is decided *for that
club year*, and it cannot again be brought up, except
by unanimous consent, until the next club year.
See section 86.

78. **Technical Reconsideration.** In consequence of the effect of the motion to reconsider
when defeated, there has grown into use another
kind of reconsideration, the *object* of which is directly opposite to that of genuine reconsideration,
though its effect is the same. While a genuine
motion to reconsider is made in good faith, for
the purpose of gaining fresh discussion and another vote, the technical or disingenuous motion
to reconsider is made for the purpose of preventing fresh discussion, by closing the matter
at once.

In other words, it checkmates a possible genuine
reconsideration by clinching the vote, and **thus**

closing the matter for good. Unlike the genuine motion, which, in common with other motions, is made by a person who wishes it to pass, this motion is made by one who wishes it to be defeated, and desires the matter not to be really reconsidered, but to be ended. A member of the party which has carried or defeated a measure will make a motion to reconsider immediately after the vote has passed; her constituents will then join with her to defeat it, and thus, by denying the reconsideration, clinch the vote and secure at once their object, safe from reversal.

79. **When the Motion to Reconsider is Made.** This motion is made only at the same session, or at the session following the one, at which the vote it relates to was taken.[1] If made at the same session, it may be considered at once, or, by motion and vote, postponed to the next session; if made at the second session, it is considered at once. It does not follow, however, in either case, that the measure shall be at once decided. If the motion prevails, and the matter is re-opened, it is subject to postponement, as

[1] See Appendix.

well as to any and all other action. If the motion is lost, that decides the measure finally.

80. **Who May Move to Reconsider.** In one important respect, the motion to reconsider differs from other motions. Other motions may be made by any member of the meeting, while this particular motion may be made *only by a member who voted with the prevailing side.* The chief reason for this restriction is that after a matter is decided, it is not fair to the party which has decided it, that they should be made liable to the danger of a reconsideration when they may be deficient in numbers. A member of the defeated side would naturally wish to get another vote, and be ready to move a reconsideration when the prevailing side was weak. It seems fair, therefore, that only a member of the successful party shall have this privilege. Furthermore, if there is some good reason for re-opening a question, it will be easy for the minority to persuade a member of the prevailing party to move to reconsider, for the sake of fairness. The rule is therefore a good one, because it works fairly for both sides. In voting *by ballot,* however, it cannot be enforced.

The general supposition is that every question is fully discussed and fairly voted upon in the first place, and that only for some excellent reason should it be re-opened. Restrictions are for protection, and to guard against surprises. This restriction prevails generally in legislatures and large assemblies; it seems to the author to be a correct principle, supported by reason and justice, and it is therefore recommended. If thought undesirable by any society, however, a special rule may be adopted to the effect that the motion to reconsider may be made by any member. It should be added also, that certain authorities teach that, *in absence of a special rule*, any member may move to reconsider, whether of the prevailing side or not. Like all other parliamentary rules which are not yet so firmly established as to become absolutely binding, this rule may be adopted or not, and any society, in deciding the matter, will follow the authority it adopts as its guide; or it may make special rules for itself. There is a conflict of opinions upon it.

81. A Possible Compromise of Conflicting Opinions. A compromise between these two methods seems to the writer to be desirable; and in the hope that some such compromise may ultimately be adopted to take their place, the following is suggested as a good rule: *a motion to reconsider, when made at the same meeting at which the vote is taken, may be moved by any member; when made at the succeeding meeting, it may be made only by a member of the prevailing side.* This would guard against surprise at the succeeding meeting, and, at the same time, make possible the introduction of new arguments at the time. The necessity for these could be shown in the debate upon the motion to reconsider. Any organization which favors this "compromise" can adopt it by special rule, and act accordingly.

82. Debate upon Reconsideration. The debate upon this motion, like the debate upon the previous question, is limited as to time, the obvious reason being that there will be little to say except why a reconsideration of the question is needful. If the debate encroaches too much upon the main question, however, the speaker is called to order. It is also true that the previous question may be ordered upon the motion to reconsider, as upon all other independent motions, thus cutting off all debate whatever. If this is done, it is a pretty sure indication that the majority do not wish to hear any more, and have made up their minds not to reconsider.

83. The "Prevailing Side." The "prevailing side" is not necessarily the affirmative side or the majority. If the motion or proposition is defeated, it is one of the negative voters who is of the prevailing side, and who may move the reconsideration. In the case of a two-thirds vote being necessary to carry a measure, if the measure is defeated, it is one of the minority who is of the prevailing side. In case of a tie vote, one of those who voted "No" is of the prevailing side, and where a unanimous vote is necessary, and is not secured, one who prevented unanimity is of the prevailing side; even if it be but one person, she alone can move the reconsideration. The prevailing side is the side that wins.

84. Illustration of Reconsideration. The Mendon Women's Club has passed the motion "that the club hold a public meeting." The vote has been regularly taken and recorded, and presumably the matter is ended. Mrs. Allen thinks that the matter has been hastily decided, or wishes to give some reasons why the project is not feasible at that time. Either at the same meeting or at the following one, she obtains the floor, and says: "Mrs. President, I move a reconsideration of the vote by which our club has voted to hold a public meeting." She then sits, and the president says: "A reconsideration can be moved only by a member of the prevailing side. If Mrs. Allen voted for this measure, the motion is in order; otherwise not." Then, if a yea and nay vote had been taken, the record is scanned to see if Mrs. Allen was on the prevailing side. If there is no recorded vote by names, Mrs. Allen will reply: "I voted with the prevailing side," or, "I did not vote with the prevailing side," as the case may be. If she did not, her motion is not in order, and unless some member of the prevailing side, out of courtesy for her, renews the motion for her, it is not stated by the chair. It would be still better for Mrs. Allen to say: "Mrs. President, I voted with the prevailing side upon (so and so), and I now move a reconsideration of that vote."

If Mrs. Allen voted with the prevailing side, the chair says: "A motion is made to reconsider the vote whereby the club decided to hold a public meeting. Are you ready? [*A limited debate may follow, confined strictly to giving reasons why the question should or should not be re-opened for debate.*] Those in favor of reconsideration will say 'Aye;' * * those opposed, 'No.' * * It is carried. The vote is reconsidered, and the subject is again before you for discussion." If the noes are in the majority, the chair will say instead: "The noes have it. The motion to reconsider is lost, and the vote to hold a public meeting stands."

85. Votes that Cannot be Reconsidered. Votes upon the following motions, whether decided affirmatively or negatively, cannot be reconsidered at all: to adjourn, to lay upon the table, for the previous question, to commit (after the committee has gone to work), to reconsider; also, appeals, elections, and ballots. Of course, no vote can be reconsidered which has been *acted upon.*

86. Reconsideration to be Sparingly Employed. Mr. Fish, in his "Guide to the Conduct of Meetings," says: "The motion to reconsider is of American origin, and is properly used only when the object cannot be attained in any other way." It is best, in other words, to do all the debating that is necessary before the vote is taken, and to consider every question fully and fairly, so that there will be no excuse for reconsideration. If this is done, there will be little need for reconsideration; it will then be employed only in emergencies, and therefore, as has been said, the motion may well be restricted to the prevailing side.

Akin to the motion "to reconsider" is the motion "to rescind;" indeed, the two terms are sometimes used synonymously. More properly, "to reconsider" means: to consider again with a view to more careful action and another vote on the question, while "to rescind" means: to reverse, or finally cancel certain action previously taken. The former motion is subject to the restrictions already noted, and when it prevails it simply re-opens the question, which is then voted upon again — thus involving two votes. The latter is an independent motion, may be made by any one, and when it prevails, is conclusive, without a second vote upon the question to be rescinded. In short, the former re-opens the matter to the action of the meeting, while the latter does not.

It is obvious that the restrictions put upon the motion to reconsider cannot be evaded by a motion to rescind, otherwise the protection secured by these restrictions would be of no avail. Such an evasion would be unfair. It follows that after the time has expired within which a matter can be reconsidered, it cannot be re-opened by a motion "to rescind." But, since no rule must be so strict as to leave no loophole of escape, it is provided that action taken in *one* club year can be rescinded the *next* club year. And further, that, by *unanimous consent*, there may be a motion to reconsider, or to rescind, after the time has expired, or after there has been already one motion.

The motion to reconsider is decided by a majority vote, whether the matter upon which it is moved required a majority, or more or less than a majority. The motion to rescind requires the same vote as did the subject it is proposed to rescind.

Form for rescinding: —

"I move to rescind the action taken on (date) in regard to (repeating the subject-matter)." This is debated and voted upon. If it prevails, the action is annulled; if it is lost, the action is re-affirmed for that club year.

Enough has been said of this matter to suffice for ordinary use. Those who may wish to study it further are referred to chapter fourteen of Cushing's manual, *sections 71–80* of Warrington's manual, and chapter twenty of Crocker's Parliamentary Procedure, second edition.

SUMMARY

A vote, having been taken and declared, is settled, unless, at the same or the next succeeding session, it is, by vote, considered again.

The effect of the motion to reconsider, if carried, is to cancel the vote and re-open the question for discussion and a second vote. Its effect, if lost, is to close the question for good.

No vote can be twice reconsidered.

The motion to reconsider may be made only by a member who voted with the prevailing party. But, as some authorities say it may be made by any member, a good rule for assemblies to make would be a compromise between these positions, allowing any member to make the motion when made the same day, and only a member of the prevailing side to make it when it is made at the succeeding session.

The motion to reconsider may be debated for a limited time.

The "prevailing party" may be the affirmative or the negative side; it is the side that *prevails*, or by which the matter is decided.

A vote cannot be reconsidered after it has influenced subsequent action. Certain technical motions are not open to reconsideration.

Reconsideration is to be used only as a last resort.

Propositions would better be fully discussed before they are decided, than to be re-opened by reconsideration.

When a matter has been properly decided by vote, and once reconsidered, it cannot again be introduced, in the same club year, without unanimous consent.

A motion to rescind is properly made when it is desired to reverse action taken a previous year.

PART III

AMENDMENT

CHAPTER XI

NATURE AND EFFECT OF AMENDMENT

NATURE OF AMENDMENT; AMENDMENTS MUST BE
GERMANE; EFFECT OF A MOTION TO AMEND;
PRIMARY AND SECONDARY AMENDMENT; ILLUS-
TRATION ; MORE THAN ONE AMENDMENT AT
ONCE; GIVING NOTICE; ACCEPTING THE AMEND-
MENT.

87. Nature of Amendment. Thus far, we
have considered the simple motion, one not altered
in any way, but voted upon in its original form.
With the complex motion, the mode of procedure
is the same. It is made, stated, put, withdrawn,
debated, and reconsidered in the same way as the
simple one. A motion, however, may be altered,
enlarged, or changed into an entirely different one,
and the process of altering the form and sense of
a motion is called "amendment." The legitimate
use of amendment, as its name implies, is "to
make better" the matter under consideration;

but, since minds differ as to what is better, the real practice of amending is to alter in any way, even if thereby the purpose of the measure or the intent of the mover is contradicted.[1]

88. Amendments Must be Germane. There is one restriction upon amendment. Any proposed change must be "germane," or relevant, to the original measure. No matter how hostile it may be; if it is germane, it is permissible. But if it is on a different *subject*, it is ruled out of order, either by the chair or by a point of order, as "not germane." An amendment also must not be "obviously trivial," or foolish. *Illustrations:* The Mendon Women's Club has under consideration a motion "That the treasurer be instructed to ascertain the price of the several halls in town, with a view to securing a permanent place of meeting for the club." Mrs. Burns moves to amend by striking out the words "the treasurer" and inserting the words "the president;" or, to amend by adding, after the word "halls," the words "and vestries;" or, to amend by striking out all after the word "instructed" and inserting instead, the

[1] See Appendix.

words "to hire a hall for a permanent place of
meeting." All these are relevant amendments,
though, as will be seen, they change the intent
of the original motion. But suppose Mrs. Burns
should move to amend by striking out the words:
"a permanent place of meeting for the club," and
inserting the words: "a place for a public enter-
tainment ;" this would be irrelevant and would
be ruled out of order as "not germane," because it
is an entirely different question. The chair would
say: "The motion of Mrs. Burns to amend by inserting the words 'a place for a public entertain-
ment,' instead of the words 'a permanent place
of meeting' is out of order, the proposed amendment not being germane to the subject under consideration, which is the finding of a place for our
regular meetings and not the holding of an enter-
tainment."

Again, if Mrs. Burns had moved that the word
" Vermont " be inserted in place of the word
"town," this would be ruled out of order as "obviously trivial." The general practice in regard
to this matter is thus concisely stated in the rule
of the United States House of Representatives:

"No motion or proposition on a subject different from that under consideration shall be admitted under color of amendment," and Warrington adds: "A member who offers a proposition in good faith is entitled to a vote upon it unembarrassed by other *subjects*, though he must submit to hostile amendments on the same general subject." There is no hardship in admitting amendments which change the intent of the motion, for "the assembly is supposed to know what it wants, and will reject them if it desires to do so."

89. **Effect of a Motion to Amend.** The effect of an offered amendment is to place two motions before the assembly, the motion to amend and the main question. And, *since a question must be perfected before it is put to vote*, the amendment is first considered and voted upon ; and then, when that is decided, the main question, "as amended," is discussed and voted upon.

Illustration : The motion in *section 68* being under consideration, Mrs. Paine obtains the floor and says: "I move to amend by inserting, after the word 'halls,' the words 'and vestries.'" The chair says: "You hear the motion to insert the words 'and vestries,' after the word 'halls,' so that the motion would read: that the treasurer is instructed to learn the price of the several halls and vestries, etc." Debate follows, *upon the amendment only*, and it is then put to vote, like any other motion. If it is adopted, the words "and vestries" become a part of the main question, and when the vote is finally taken upon that, the chair will say: "The question is now upon the original motion as amended. The motion is as follows." [*She repeats it in its present form, with whatever amendments have been incorporated in it, and then puts it to vote.*]

90. **Primary and Secondary Amendment.** Besides the one amendment, there may also be offered *an amendment to an amendment;* that is, a modification of the amendment may be proposed, which bears the same relation to it, as it, in turn, bears to the main question. In this case, the former may be called the "primary," and the latter the "secondary" amendment. The former is an amendment to the original motion; the latter is an amendment to the amendment, and, through it, to the original motion. The secondary amendment is first

decided (because the primary amendment, before being voted upon, is to be perfected), and the vote is then taken upon "the amendment as amended." There are thus three motions to be put to vote: 1. The vote on the secondary; 2. The vote on the primary; 3. The vote on the perfected main question.

This is as far as the amending can go; there can be no amendment to an amendment to an amendment, because confusion would result.

After one amendment is decided upon, whether it be adopted or defeated, another may be offered, then another, and another, and so on. This is true of both the primary and the secondary amendment. The reason for this is because after the amendment is voted upon, there remains only the one question (or the two in case of the secondary) before the meeting, and the restriction in regard to amending extends only to *forbidding more than three motions at a time:* 1. The original; 2. The primary amendment; 3. The secondary amendment. Therefore, as soon as one secondary is disposed of, the way is left open for another, and so on. The principle is that *an amendment, if adopted, becomes an integral part of the motion to which it relates,* which motion then takes on the new form, and is considered in the new form as if it were that originally; one amendment with its secondaries being disposed of, another may be moved and then another, until the original motion is in the form desired by the majority; and then it is put to vote.

91. **Illustration of Primary and Secondary Amendment.**[1] The Mendon Women's Club has under consideration the motion "that the club establish a library of books and magazines for the use of the members." The chair has placed the motion before the club, and it has been discussed. Mrs. Robbins wishes to offer an amendment, and the following process is followed: —

Mrs. Robbins (rising). Mrs. President.

The Chair (rising). Mrs. Robbins.

Mrs. Robbins. I move to amend this motion by inserting the word "newspapers" after the word "magazines"[2] (*sits*).

The Chair. You hear the motion of Mrs. Robbins; to insert the word "newspapers" after the word

---

[1] See Appendix.

[2] It is to be noted that she says "the word newspapers," and not simply "newspapers."

"magazines," so that the motion would read — "a library of books, magazines, and newspapers." Are you ready for the question?

Mrs. Paine. Mrs. President.

The Chair. Mrs. Paine.

Mrs. Paine. I move to amend this amendment by inserting the word "weekly" before the word "newspapers."

The Chair. Mrs. Paine moves to insert the word "weekly" before the word "newspapers." Are you ready? [1] [*Debate follows upon the insertion of the word "weekly."*]

The Chair. The first question is upon the motion to amend the amendment, by inserting the word "weekly." Those in favor will say "Aye;" * * those opposed, "No." * * It is a vote. The question now comes upon the amendment as amended; namely, the insertion of the words "and weekly newspapers" after the word "magazines." Are you

---

[1] In order to make it more clear, the chair may repeat each amendment, as it would read if amended. For instance: "Mrs. Paine moves to amend the amendment by inserting the word 'weekly' before the word 'newspapers,' so that the primary amendment would read: 'to insert the words "weekly newspapers";' are you ready?" The idea is to keep each stage distinct in the mind, and to so state it to the meeting that there will be no confusion as to just what they are voting upon.

ready to vote? [*Debate upon the amendment as amended.*] Those in favor will say "Aye;" * * those opposed, "No." * * It is carried, and the words are inserted. The question now comes upon the original motion as amended; namely, "that the club establish a library of books, magazines, and weekly newspapers for the use of the members." Are there any further amendments? [*If there are, they are moved in the same way.*] If not, those in favor of the motion in its present amended form will say "Aye." * * *

It will be noted that the debate is restricted to the question directly before the meeting. This is an elastic rule, however, and when an amendment, or its secondary, is closely related to the main question, the debate will necessarily extend to the whole question, and a presiding officer will seldom enforce the restriction, though she may do so, and should, when in her judgment the two propositions are sufficiently distinct.

92. **More than One Amendment at Once.** It is the practice in experienced bodies, sometimes to admit, at the same time, more than one primary amendment, each one being related to a

different part of the main question. But in inexperienced societies, it is better to observe the
general practice of admitting only one at a time,
acting upon that, and then admitting others, one
by one. Mr. Crocker well expresses this practice
in the following words: "When an amendment is
pending, another amendment cannot be entertained
unless such subsequent amendment is an amendment to the pending amendment."

Illustration: In the motion quoted above, in
section 91, Mrs. Robbins, having moved to amend
by inserting the word "newspapers," and that
motion being before the meeting, Miss Lovell
moves to amend by striking out the word "members," and inserting the word "public." The
chair will say, in this case: "Only one amendment can be considered at a time. Miss Lovell's
motion is not now in order, the question being
upon Mrs. Robbins's motion, which must first be
decided." Miss Lovell's motion introduced a new
proposition, which, not being "an amendment to
the pending amendment," is not then in order.

93. **Giving Notice.** When one wishes to offer
an amendment which is not then in order, she

may "give notice" that she intends so to do when there is opportunity. This will prepare the way for her motion; and the assembly, thus notified of her intent, may vote differently upon the matter before them.

Illustration: Miss Lovell having made the motion, as in *section 92,* and the chair having ruled it out of order, Miss Lovell may proceed to say: "I desire to give notice, then, that at the proper time I shall move to insert the word 'public' in place of the word 'members.'" She then sits, the consideration of Mrs. Robbins's motion proceeds, and when that is decided, Miss Lovell obtains the floor and offers her amendment, the way being now clear.

This method of giving notice is specially valuable when one secondary amendment has been offered, and some one wishes to offer another. The latter, being out of order till the former is voted upon, notice of it will often change the vote upon the former. For example, suppose Miss Lovell wishes to have the word "daily" inserted, instead of the word "weekly," before the word "newspapers." (*See section 91.*) She cannot make that as a motion, because already a primary and a secondary amendment are under consideration. But she may give notice, saying: " I desire to give notice that if the motion to insert the word 'weekly' is rejected, I shall move to insert the word 'daily,' " thus giving a hint to any others who may prefer " daily," that they may vote against " weekly."

94. Accepting the Amendment. The simplest way of disposing of an amendment is for the mover of the motion to "accept" the proposed amendment. In case of objection, however, an amendment cannot be so "accepted," it being in the possession of the assembly after being stated by the chair. When an amendment is accepted, it becomes a part of the motion, as if the mover had originally included it, and is not separately voted upon. Of course the mover will accept an amendment only when she favors it; if she disapproves of it, she simply remains silent, and the amendment takes its proper course as a separate proposition, succeeding or failing on its own merits. The chair should not *ask* if the amendment is accepted. An amendment is not "lost" by not being accepted, but is regularly put to vote.

Illustration: The motion in regard to the library of books and magazines (*see section 91*) being before the club, Mrs. Burns moves "to amend by inserting the word 'newspapers' after the word 'magazines.'" During the discussion, Mrs. Packard moves "to amend the amendment by inserting the word 'weekly' before the word 'newspapers.'" Mrs. Burns, if she favors this, may rise and say: "Mrs. President, I accept the amendment." If no one makes objection, the motion then becomes: "to amend by inserting the words 'weekly newspapers,'" and as such it is stated by the chair and voted upon. A further restriction is that a motion, or an amendment to it, cannot be accepted after it has been changed in any way. If, for instance, Mrs. Burns's motion to amend by inserting "newspapers" had been further amended by adding "pamphlets," it would no longer be in her power to accept Mrs. Packard's motion to insert "weekly."

SUMMARY

An amendment is any change *in meaning* which is proposed to the question under discussion.

It may alter the proposition in any way, provided it is "germane," or relevant, to it.

The effect of a motion to amend is to place two motions before the meeting, the motion to amend and the motion to be amended.

The amendment is considered and voted upon first; the vote is then taken on the "motion as amended."

"Besides the amendment to the motion, there may be also an amendment to the amendment. These are then called the "primary" and the "secondary" amendment.

The secondary amendment is decided first; the vote is then taken upon the "amendment as amended," and lastly, upon the " motion as amended."

There can be no tertiary amendment.

After one amendment, either primary or secondary, is decided, another may be offered, and so on.

An amendment, when adopted, becomes an integral part of the motion.

One amendment, with its secondaries, is disposed of before another is entertained.

"Notice" of other amendments may be given while one is pending.

The mover of the original motion may, if there is no objection, "accept" an amendment; it then becomes a part of her motion. The same is true of a secondary amendment.

Failure to accept an amendment does not defeat the amendment.

CHAPTER XII

WAYS TO AMEND A PROPOSITION

THE THREE WAYS OF AMENDING; FORMS FOR
STATING THE QUESTION; THE METHOD BY IN-
SERTING; EFFECT OF A NEGATIVE VOTE ON IN-
SERTION; A CHANGE IN MEANING NECESSARY;
THE METHOD BY STRIKING OUT; EFFECT OF A
NEGATIVE VOTE ON STRIKING OUT; FORM FOR
PUTTING TO VOTE; REJECTED WORDS IN A
DIFFERENT PLACE; THE WORD "NOT"; THE
METHOD BY STRIKING OUT AND INSERTING;
EFFECT OF A NEGATIVE VOTE ON STRIKING OUT
AND INSERTING; SUBSTITUTION.

95. **The Three Ways of Amending.** A
motion may be made to amend a motion, or proposition, in three ways: 1. By inserting words;
2. By striking out words; 3. By striking out
words and inserting other words in their place.

Illustrations: 1. *Inserting.* The motion "that
the club establish a library of books and magazines
for the use of the members" being under discus-

sion, Mrs. Ellis moves "to amend by inserting the word 'circulating' before the word 'library';" or, "to amend by inserting the words 'and their friends' after the word 'members';" or, "to amend by inserting the word 'newspapers' after the word 'magazines.'" 2. *Striking Out.* In the same matter, Miss Sawyer moves "to amend the motion by striking out the words 'and magazines,'" or, "to amend by striking out the words 'for the use of the members.'" 3. *Striking Out and Inserting.* Mrs. Paine moves "to amend by striking out the words 'the members' and inserting the words 'the public';" or, "to amend by striking out the words 'books and magazines,' and inserting the words 'periodicals and newspapers.'" Each of these is a primary amendment, and each may be amended secondarily, one at a time.

96. **Forms for Stating the Question.** The chair, in putting an amendment to vote, not only repeats the amendment, but also states how the question will stand if amended. The three forms are as follows: 1. "It is moved to amend by inserting the words —— after the words ——, so that the motion would read ——." 2. "It is

moved to strike out after the word —— the words
——, so that the motion would read ——." 3. "It
is moved to strike out the words ——, and insert
in their place the words ——, so that the motion
would read ——."

97. **The Method by Inserting.** Any words
relevant to the subject may be inserted by a majority
vote. Once inserted, the same identical words, or
a part of them, cannot afterward be stricken out,
except by a reconsideration, the rule being, that
the same matter cannot twice be acted upon. But, certain words having once been inserted, other words
may be added to them by another amendment; and
then the whole can be stricken out by still another
motion to amend.

Illustration : The motion "that the club establish a library of books and magazines for the use
of the members" being under consideration, the
following action takes place : —

Mrs. Paine (after obtaining the floor), I move
to insert the word "circulating" before the word
"library."

The Chair. You hear the motion of Mrs. Paine,
to insert the word "circulating," before the word

"library," so that the motion would read: "that the club establish a *circulating* library," etc. Are you ready for the question? * * * Those in favor will say "Aye." * * * Those opposed, "No." * * * It is a vote. Are there any further amendments?

Mrs. Robbins (after obtaining the floor), I move to insert the word "free" before the word "circulating," so that it would read: "free circulating library for the use of the members."

The Chair. You hear the motion: to amend by inserting the word "free," so that the motion before you would read as follows: [*she repeats it.*] Those in favor * * * It is carried.

Mrs. Robbins. I now move to strike out the words "free circulating" before the word "library." [*The chair repeats and puts this motion to vote.*]

The object of Mrs. Robbins in making her two motions was to get another vote upon Mrs. Paine's amendment to insert the word "circulating," with a view to defeating it. The amendment having once been carried could not be voted upon again, except by a reconsideration; and the result of this might be uncertain. Mrs. Robbins therefore secured another vote, and so another chance of defeating it, by moving to add the word "free," and then, this being adopted, by moving to strike out the whole. She thus secured two opportunities for debate and two votes, and doubled the chance of defeating the motion she objected to. Mrs. Paine's motion, of course, was made with no ulterior motive in view.

The reason why this double action is permissible is because the new word "free," added to the adopted amendment, made of it a *different question*. It could then be acted upon regardless of the fact that it had already once been acted upon — the restriction being only that *the same matter, or a part of it, cannot be stricken out by amendment when once inserted.*

98. Effect of a Negative Vote for Inserting. Conversely, if certain words are proposed to be inserted, and the motion to amend in this way is *rejected*, those same words, or a part of them, cannot be afterward added. But a motion can be made to add the same words, or a part of them, *with other words;* this being a different proposition. In the motion under consideration, if Mrs. Paine had moved to insert the word "newspapers," and her motion had been rejected, she could afterward move to insert the words "religious newspapers" or "periodicals bearing upon women's work," this being a new question, which, while embodying her defeated amendment, also includes other matter, and thus makes a different proposition.

99. **A Change in Meaning Necessary.** It is important to note that mere verbal changes are not enough to make of the rejected motion a "new proposition." The added words must change the meaning, or scope, of the rejected amendment, else it will be the same matter, and as such cannot twice be acted upon. Mrs. Paine could not have moved to insert "daily newspapers," because these words are in meaning (though not verbally) the same as the word "newspapers," and that had already been rejected; but "periodicals bearing upon women's work" or "religious newspapers" is a different matter from "newspapers;" and the club might be willing to vote for such a limited proposition, while opposed to the more general one.

100. **The Method by Striking Out.** The motion to amend by striking out is so closely allied to the motion to amend by inserting, that the consideration of the one almost necessarily in-

volves that of the other. The same rules apply. Any words may be stricken out; but the same matter, or a part of it, having once been stricken out, cannot be added again except by reconsideration. The words stricken out, or a part of them, can afterward be added *provided* other material is combined with them so as to make a different proposition.

Illustration : The same motion being under consideration, Miss Sawyer moves "to amend by striking out the words 'and magazines.'" The chair states the motion, puts it to vote, and it is carried. These identical words ("and magazines") are now stricken out for good, unless there is a reconsideration. But it may happen that Miss Lovell is opposed to their being stricken out, and wishes to get them in again. She may move "to amend by inserting the words 'pamphlets and periodicals bearing upon our work.'" This will include certain magazines, but is not a motion to insert the word "magazines" alone, and is therefore a different proposition from the one already acted upon.

101. Effect of a Negative Vote on Striking Out. Conversely, if a motion to strike out certain words is *lost*, those identical words stand as an integral part of the motion, and cannot again be acted upon without reconsideration. But a motion can be made to strike out these words, or a part of them, *with others*, this being a new proposition. In the illustration in *section 100*, if Miss Sawyer's motion to amend by striking out "magazines" had been lost, she could afterward move "to strike out the words 'books and magazines,'" because this, while it includes the rejected motion, is really a different one. To repeat, in the words of Mr. Crocker: "A proposition which has once been acted upon, cannot be renewed as an amendment."

102. Form for Putting to Vote the Motion to Strike Out. Motions are usually put to vote in the form in which they are made, the chair exactly repeating the motion. According to Cushing,[1] the motion to strike out differs in this particular from others. The chair, in putting the motion to vote says : " The motion is to strike out after the word 'books' the words 'and magazines.' Shall the words 'and magazines' *stand* as a part of the mo-

---

[1] Thomas B. Reed, on the contrary, in his " Rules," says: " It is moved that the following words (stating them) in such a place (describing it) be stricken out, and the question is, Will the assembly agree to the amendment?"

tion?" This gives the advantage of the affirmative vote to the *opponents* of the measure, reversing
the usual effect of a vote, which is to give the
affirmative advantage to the affirmative side.

It is not easy to see any good reason for this
exception, and it is not sanctioned by Warrington,
Fish, or Crocker. It is also somewhat confusing to
beginners. For these reasons, it is not recommended here. The form recommended is as follows : —

The Chair. The motion is made to strike out,
after the word "library," the words "books and
magazines." Shall these words be stricken out?
Those in favor * * * It is a vote."

103. Rejected Words in a Different Place.
Words once rejected (either by an affirmative vote
on a motion to strike out, or by a negative vote on
a motion to insert) may sometimes be inserted into
the main proposition in a different place. This can
happen only when the main question has been materially altered by amendment, so that new consid-
erations have become involved, and the meaning
of the text has been changed.

104. The Word "Not." An amendment to

insert or to strike out the word "not," so as to make the motion its exact opposite, is not admissible, and is to be ruled out of order. The same is true of any other words which simply negative the words under discussion, like "impossible" for "possible," etc. When it is desired to negative a motion, the proper way is to vote against it when it is acted upon.

105. The Method by Striking Out and Inserting. Any words may be stricken out of a proposition, and any others, relevant thereto, may be inserted in their place. Having been inserted, they can be stricken out only under the conditions explained in *section 100.* The motion "to strike out and insert" is *one motion;* it is a combination, so to speak, of the motion "to strike out" and the motion "to insert," and is a motion "to strike out A, and insert B." It cannot be divided into two motions (one to strike out A, and another to insert B), either by the chair or by a vote; but, having been made as one motion, is put as one motion. The reason for this is because the mover has a right to have a vote upon the words she wishes *to take the place* of the words she wishes stricken out.

If the motion could be divided (words being stricken out and the place left blank), other words than those she desires might then get inserted instead, thus thwarting her intention. Therefore, *the motion to strike out and insert is indivisible.*

Illustration : The motion " to establish a library of books and magazines for the use of the members," being under consideration, Miss Faxon obtains the floor and says : " I move to strike out the word ' members ' and insert the word 'public.' "

The Chair. You hear the motion of Miss Faxon, to strike out the word " members " and insert the word "public," so that the motion would read " a library, etc., for the use of the public." Are you ready for the question ? * * * Those in favor of striking out the word " members," and inserting in its place the word " public," will say " Aye." * * * If the motion prevails, the word " public" becomes a part of the original motion, instead of the word " members." Any one who wishes to get the word "public " out, must either move a reconsideration, or proceed as described in *section 100.*

106. **Effect of a Negative Vote for Striking Out and Inserting.** If the motion to strike out

certain words and insert others is defeated, the
original words stand, and must continue to stand,
unless the motion is reconsidered. But, by incor-
porating other matter with the original words, and
thus making a different proposition, the same
words may again, indirectly, be acted upon by
amendment.

In order to get a second vote on words already
acted upon (by this motion to strike out and insert)
certain motions may be made; these, as formulated
by Cushing are substantially as follows:—

1. To strike out (*without inserting*).

2. To strike out the same words and insert *different* ones from those before proposed.

3. To strike out the same words and insert the
proposed words, *with others*.

4. To strike out the same words and insert *part*
of the proposed words, *with others*.

5. To strike out the same words *with others* and
insert the proposed words.

6. To strike out *part* of the same words *with
others* and insert the proposed words.

7. To strike out *other words* and insert the proposed words.

8. To insert the desired words (*without striking out*).

It would be difficult to illustrate all these methods by one motion, and probably in no single motion could all of them be used. They are expedients, some one of which may often be employed, in an attempt to reverse the decision upon a rejected motion to strike out and insert, and thus to get rid of words which, by vote, have been retained.

A motion to amend by striking out and inserting, having once been acted upon, the same proposition cannot again be introduced.

107. Substitution. A whole new motion may be substituted for another already before the meeting, provided the subject of it be germane to that other. This, being simply a motion to strike out and insert, is put as one motion.

Illustration: The motion in regard to a library being under discussion, Mrs. Ellis says: "I move to amend by substituting for the pending motion the following: "That during the summer the president ascertain the probable expense of a library suitable to our needs, and that contributions for that purpose be solicited." The chair says: "It is moved to substitute for the motion now before us (which is, 'To establish a library of books and magazines for the use of the members') the following motion: 'That during the summer the president ascertain the probable expense of a library suitable to our needs; and that contributions be solicited.'"

The question now is upon *substituting* one for the other. The proposed substitute, being simply an amendment, may be amended before the vote is taken upon substitution; it may also be divided, since it contains two distinct propositions. It is debated, like any other amendment, and finally voted upon (in its original form, or as further amended), and if the vote is in the affirmative, the substitute *takes the place of the original motion.* This vote is the vote upon it *as the amendment.* Another vote is then taken upon it as *the motion as amended.*

These two votes are put in the following form: 1. "Those in favor of substituting this motion for the pending one will say 'Aye.' * * * It is carried, and the motion is substituted. 2. Those now in favor of the motion as amended ('that the president ascertain, etc.') will say 'Aye' * * * It is carried."

SUMMARY

A proposition may be amended: 1. By inserting;
2. By striking out; 3. By striking out and inserting.

In stating the motion to amend, the chair (1)
repeats the words proposed; (2) indicates the place
in the motion where they are proposed to be inserted, or omitted; and (3) reads the motion in the
form it will stand if amended.

Any words relevant to the subject may be inserted. Once inserted, the same words, or a part of
them, cannot be stricken out; but other words may
be added to them, and then the whole be stricken
out.

If a motion to amend by inserting is negatived,
the same words or a part of them cannot afterward
be added. But the same words, or a part of them,
with others, may be added.

The added words must change the meaning, and
not produce a mere verbal change.

Any words may be stricken out. Once out, they
cannot afterward be inserted, unless other words are
added to them.

If a motion to amend by striking out is negatived,

the words stand, and cannot afterward be acted upon unless combined with others.

The motion to strike out is put: Shall the words be stricken out? and *not* Shall the words stand?

Rejected words may sometimes be inserted in a different place.

The word "not," or any other word which simply negatives the meaning of a motion, cannot be offered in amendment.

A motion may be made to strike out any words and to insert any others, relevant thereto, in their place. This is one motion.

The motion to strike out and insert is indivisible.

When the motion to strike out and insert is negatived, the original words stand, but they may afterward be stricken out, by a motion which changes either the words to be stricken out, or the words to be inserted.

A whole new motion may be substituted for another, provided it is relevant thereto.

Rule: *The same proposition cannot twice be acted upon by amendment.*

CHAPTER XIII

EXCEPTIONS REGARDING AMENDMENT

Sums and Times, or Filling Blanks; Names; Motions not Subject to Amendment; Effect of the Previous Question ; Reconsideration; The Order in Amending.

108. Sums and Times, or Filling Blanks. There is one apparent exception to the rule that a proposition cannot be amended beyond the second degree (that is, that there can be no amendment to an amendment to an amendment). In case a *number* is in question, and it is proposed to change it to some other number, as many suggestions are received as the members wish to offer, and then these suggestions are voted upon, one by one, in a certain order, the rule that the second takes precedence of the first not applying here.

The number to be supplied is usually a sum (of money) or a time (of day), and when a motion is made, or a proposition offered, which contains reference to a sum or a time, and there is any mo-

tion to change that sum or time, such a motion is
not regarded as an amendment, but the space containing the number is considered to be blank or
empty, and suggestions are then received for filling it. These suggestions are noted down by the
chairman or secretary, and then the vote is taken
upon each, one by one, beginning with the largest
sum, or the longest time, and continuing down until an affirmative vote is reached on some one of
the numbers proposed. This same process is also
followed whenever there is before a meeting any
proposition containing a blank space to be filled
by a sum or a time.

Illustration: A motion is made "that the time
for the club to assemble be fixed at two o'clock."

The chair having placed the motion before the
meeting, Mrs. Paine obtains the floor and moves
"that the hour be three o'clock; " (*not* "to amend
by striking out 'two' and inserting 'three.')"

The Chair. We will proceed as in filling blanks,
and the chair will receive other suggestions.

Mrs. Packard. I move that the hour be half-
past two.

Mrs. Burns. I move that it be half-past three.

Miss Long. I move that it be four, Mrs. President.

The Chair. The motion is in regard to the hour of meeting of our club. Motions have been made that the hour be two, three, half-past two, half-past three, and four o'clock. These motions are before you for discussion. (*The suggestions are debated.*)

The Chair. Are you ready for the question? Those in favor of four o'clock will say "Aye." * * * It is lost. Those in favor of half-past three will say "Aye." * * * It is lost. Those in favor of three o'clock will say "Aye." * * * It is lost. Those in favor of half-past two o'clock will say "Aye." * * * It is carried, and the blank is filled by the insertion of the words "half-past two." Those now in favor of the motion "that the time for the club to assemble be fixed at half-past two o'clock" will say "Aye;" those opposed, "No." It is carried. The hour of assembling is half-past two.

At first thought, the taking of two votes upon the words "half-past two" seems unnecessary; but the first vote (on inserting) is a vote upon an amendment, as explained in *section 107*, and it does not necessarily follow that all those who vote for "half-past two," are also in favor of the main question. There might be members who object to fixing *any* time for assembling.

There are cases where this would be still more apparent, especially where a question of appropriating money is under consideration. Members might favor one sum rather than another, but be opposed to any appropriation. For example: a motion "to subscribe ten dollars toward the fresh-air fund" being offered, motions are offered to make the sum twenty, fifteen, and five dollars. The chair will put these to vote, beginning with the largest, and then say: "The blank is filled by the word 'fifteen.' Those now in favor of the original motion, as amended, to subscribe fifteen dollars for the fresh-air fund will say 'Aye.' * * *" Members opposed to *any* subscription would now have a chance to vote against the main question. Rule. — *A vote is first taken upon filling the blank, this being a form of amendment, and then a vote is taken upon the motion itself.*

In rare cases, the shortest number precedes the

longest, in putting to vote; but the general rule is the other way, the reason being that usually the greater number is the more inclusive, leading up, so to speak, to the others, and bringing the question more readily to a conclusion.

109. Names. Where the names of several persons are put in nomination for one office, these are not treated as amendments, but the same process is followed as that described in the preceding section in regard to sums and times. The names are put to vote in the order nominated, beginning with the one mentioned in the original motion or report; or, a ballot may be taken. For an illustration see chapter one.

110. Motions not Subject to Amendment. There are certain motions that cannot be amended. The principal ones are: to adjourn; to lay upon, and to take from, the table; for the previous question; to reconsider; to postpone indefinitely.

Rule. — *Any motion may be amended that can be amended without changing it into a motion of a different kind.* For instance: " to close debate " cannot be amended by a motion, " to close debate at a stated time."

111. Effect of the Previous Question. It may be well to repeat, that after the debate is closed, no new amendments, except verbal ones, are admissible. Changes in meaning cannot then be offered, because they cannot be discussed. Also, when an amendment is before the meeting, the debate is confined to the amendment, except in cases where such amendment necessarily opens the whole question.

112. Reconsideration. If, after a motion has been adopted, it is desired to reconsider the vote upon an amendment to that motion, the vote upon the whole question must first be reconsidered, in order to open the way for action upon the amendment.

113. The Order in Amending. As already explained, when several primary amendments to one proposition are before a meeting, they are considered in the order moved; when there is a primary and a secondary, the latter is voted upon and then the former. When there is a series of propositions combined in one, like the by-laws of a society for instance (*see section 11*), it is best to consider these section by section, amending

them in their order. It is not well, however, to
"adopt" them one by one, as this prevents the
assembly from going back and considering them
over again. This is often necessary, and, if they
are simply amended and left, it can be done at
any time before the by-laws are "adopted as a
whole." When all the amending is done and the
meeting is ready, a motion is made "to adopt the
by-laws as a whole." If this is carried, the matter is closed, not to be re-opened, except by reconsideration.

For division of motions, *see section 41.*

SUMMARY

Numbers and names are not treated as amendments. Blanks are presumed to exist, and these
are filled by voting upon the proposed numbers
or names, one by one.

The largest sum or the longest time is put to
vote first, and so on down, till one is adopted.

One vote is to be taken upon filling the blank
in the motion and another vote upon the motion
as amended, (the blank being filled.)

Names are put to vote in their order, beginning
with the one first named, or chosen by ballot.

Any motions may be amended, except such as cannot be changed without destroying their nature.

After the previous question is ordered, no amendments except verbal ones are admissible.

When an amendment is under consideration, debate is confined to that amendment, unless it necessarily involves the main question.

In order to reconsider an amendment, the main question must first be reconsidered.

When there is a series of propositions combined into one, these are amended section by section and finally adopted "as a whole."

PART IV

THE PRECEDENCE OF MOTIONS

CHAPTER XIV

THE RANK OF DEPENDENT MOTIONS

" Precedence " Defined; " Independent " *vs.* "Dependent" Motions ; The Seven Dependent Motions and Their Rank; Illustration of the Precedence of Motions; Object of the Seven Motions; Reasons for the Prescribed Order.

114. "Precedence" Defined. The word "precedence" in this connection, refers to the *order* in which motions are to be considered. The general rule is that *motions take precedence in the order moved,* the one first made being first considered and decided. There are exceptions to this rule in the case of certain motions which, from their nature, take precedence of the motion pending, and which also have a precedence, or rank, among themselves.

115. "Independent" *vs.* **"Dependent Motions."** A motion which stands for itself, unrelated to any other, and the effect of which is to place before the meeting a new question, is an "independent" motion. With all independent motions, the general rule of precedence prevails, namely, an independent motion may be made *when no other motion is pending*, and one independent motion is decided before another is in order.

A "dependent" motion is one which may be made while another is pending. It depends, or "hangs," so to speak, from the independent motion, and tends in some way to modify it or to change its status. The motions to close debate and to amend are examples of dependent motions. A dependent motion is necessarily acted upon before the independent motion to which it relates. The dependent motions have a prescribed order among themselves, certain ones taking precedence of certain others and ruling out those others even when the latter are first made.

116. **The Seven Dependent Motions and Their Rank.** There are seven dependent motions which are in constant use in the conduct of meetings; and among all the motions of this nature

which are possible in practice, these are the only ones necessary to be mastered by the ordinary parliamentarian. Two of these have been considered already in the connections where they belong: the motion to amend, which, being the most important and most common, is considered in Part III., by itself; and the motion for the previous question, which is considered in chapter eight, in connection with debate. The other five are: the motions to adjourn, to lay upon the table, to postpone to a definite time, to commit or to refer to a committee, and to postpone indefinitely or to repress. The rank of these motions is as follows: —

1. To adjourn.
2. To lay upon the table.
3. For the previous question.
4. To postpone.
5. To commit.
6. To amend.
7. To postpone indefinitely.

Each of these dependent motions takes precedence of the main question; in other words, when a proposition is pending, and one of these motions is made, that motion is considered and put to vote before the main proposition, which is interrupted. in its course by the dependent motion and variously modified thereby. *See section 157.*

When a proposition is under consideration and one of these seven motions is made, if *another of the seven* is made afterward, it can be considered *if it stands above the first one* in this list. If it stands below, it is not admissible. For example: suppose an independent motion to be under discussion, and that a motion has been made "to postpone." While this is under consideration, the motions which can *now* be made are: to adjourn, to lay on the table, and for the previous question; while those which cannot be made are: to commit, to amend, and to postpone indefinitely. The motions which stand above the dependent motion pending are said to "have precedence over it;" those below, are said to be "preceded by" it. If the independent motion (or main question) with a number of amendments, were pending, any of the dependent motions is admissible except the seventh, that only being "preceded by" motions to amend. If they all are made, in proper order, they are voted upon, one by one, in their order of precedence, the main question being held in abeyance till they are settled.

117. Illustration of the Precedence of Motions. A motion having been made "that the Mendon Women's Club take steps to become incorporated," the following action ensues: —

Mrs. Robbins.[1] I move to amend by inserting, after the word "steps," the words "during the summer vacation."

The Chair. You hear the motion, — to amend by inserting certain words so that the motion shall read: "—— take steps during the summer vacation to become incorporated." Are you ready? [*This may be debated.*]

Miss Long. I move to commit.

The Chair. It is moved to refer the matter to a committee. This motion takes precedence of the motion to amend. Are you ready to vote upon the motion to commit? [*Debatable.*]

Mrs. Paine. I move to postpone the matter for one week.

The Chair. A motion is made to postpone. [*Debatable.*]

[1] In this illustration, the form of obtaining the floor is omitted for sake of brevity. The reader must supply it.

Mrs. Burns.   I move the previous question.

The Chair.   The previous question is moved. Shall the main question be now put? [*Limited debate.*]

Mrs. Allen.   I move to lay upon the table. [*Not debatable.*]

The Chair.   It is moved to lay on the table. Those in favor —

Mrs. Packard (interrupting).   Mrs. President!

The Chair.   The motion to table is not debatable.

Mrs. Packard.   I was not intending to debate, Mrs. Chairman, but to move that we adjourn.

The Chair.   The Chair stands corrected. A motion to adjourn is now in order, that taking precedence of all other motions. The vote comes first upon the motion to adjourn. Those in favor of adjournment will say "Aye" * * * It is lost. Those in favor of laying the question upon the table * * * It is lost. The next motion is for the previous question. Shall the main question be now put? (If this prevails, it will cut off the motions to postpone and to commit, and bring us to an immediate vote on the main question and

its amendments.[1])   Those in favor *** It is lost.
Are you ready for the question upon the motion
to postpone for one week?   Those in favor * * *
It is lost.

Miss Lovell.   I move to postpone indefinitely.

The Chair.   Motions to commit and to amend
being before the meeting, the motion to postpone
indefinitely is not in order.   Are you ready to
vote upon commitment?   Those in favor * * * It
is lost.   The question now recurs upon Mrs. Robbins' motion to amend by inserting the words
"during the summer vacation."   Are you ready?
Those in favor * * * It is carried.   Those now in
favor of the motion as amended —

Miss Lovell (interrupting).   I now move to postpone indefinitely.

The Chair.   That motion is now in order.
Those in favor of repressing the motion will say
"Aye" * * * It is lost.   Those in favor of the
motion as amended, namely [*she repeats it*], will
say "Aye" * * * It is carried.

This illustration shows the effect of the depen-

[1] This explanation of the president is desirable, to prevent inexperienced members from misunderstanding the effect of their vote.   It is well
for the chairman to explain other difficult motions.

dent motions, when each one (except that to amend) is *lost.* Illustrations of the effect when each one is *carried* are given in the three following chapters. When any one of them is moved and is not in order because of the precedence of others, it is treated as shown in Miss Lovell's motion to postpone indefinitely.

Any of these motions, having once been defeated, may again be made at a later stage in the proceedings, provided "substantial business" has intervened in the meantime. For example, another motion to table might have been made at the close; or between the consideration of any other two motions. So with the other dependent motions, subject always to the rule of precedence. Only the dependent motion distinctively under consideration may be debated, unless it necessarily involves the main question.

When a motion is made which takes precedence of others, these others are simply suspended, or held in abeyance, till the one that outranks them is decided. If it is decided in the negative, they follow in their order, as shown in the illustration.

118. Object of the Seven Motions. The

object of three of these motions (to adjourn, to table, and to postpone) is to delay action; of one (to close debate), to hasten action; of two (to commit and to amend), to perfect or change; and of one, the last, to finally dispose of. For the effect of the previous question upon the other dependent motions, *see sections 60 and 61*.

119. Reasons for the Prescribed Order. This order has been found, by experience, to be well suited to secure both the fair and the speedy transaction of business. The undebatable motions precede the debatable ones, in order to prevent delays; and opportunity is given to secure, first, the temporary disposition of the subject, then the suspension of tiresome debate, then the perfecting in form and the securing of more time, and lastly, repression. The order is varied by some authorities and disregarded by others; any society may therefore vote, by special rule, not to adopt it, if they wish; but it will be found simple and helpful, and is therefore recommended. Presiding officers would do well to commit this order to memory, or to have it by them for reference when presiding.

SUMMARY

The general rule regarding precedence is that motions take precedence in the order moved. There are exceptions regarding certain technical motions.

An independent motion is one that is unrelated to any other; a dependent motion is one that exists because of an independent one. The former is made when no other motion is pending; the latter, when another is pending. The seven dependent motions in general use are: 1. To adjourn; 2. To lay on the table: 3. For the previous question; 4. To postpone; 5. To commit; 6. To amend; 7. To postpone indefinitely. These take precedence of one another in the order given.

When one of these is made, it takes precedence of the main question; when one is made, and then another, that other is admissible if its place in the list is above the one first made.

When one of these has been defeated, it may be renewed after substantial business has intervened.

Undebatable motions take precedence of debatable motions. This order has been proved by experience to facilitate both full and speedy action.

CHAPTER XV

THE MOTIONS TO ADJOURN AND TO LAY UPON THE TABLE

THE MOTION TO ADJOURN; THE INDEPENDENT
MOTION TO ADJOURN; LIMITATIONS; EFFECT OF
ADJOURNMENT; FIXING THE TIME; THE MOTION
TO LAY UPON THE TABLE; ITS EFFECT; TAKING
FROM THE TABLE.

120. **The Motion to Adjourn.** The dependent motion first in order is the motion to adjourn.
This takes precedence of all other motions. The
reason for its high rank is that the assembly
has the right, at any time, to terminate its session at the will of the majority. It is considered
at once, and decided without debate. It cannot be
amended, tabled, committed, postponed, repressed,
or reconsidered; all that can be done to it is
simply to vote upon it.

121. **The Independent Motion to Adjourn.**
Besides being dependent, the motion to adjourn is
also, at times, an independent motion. It is such

when made after all business is done, or while no
motion is pending.   It is still subject to the same
restrictions.   By unanimous consent, however, it
can be briefly debated, reasons being given why
the assembly ought not to adjourn at once.   Usually, an independent motion to adjourn is made as
a formality, at the close of a session, and will be
readily withdrawn by the mover, if any one indicates (by raising a question of privilege), that
there is business which ought to be considered.

122. **Limitations.**   It is commonly said that
"a motion to adjourn is always in order."   This is
not strictly true.   A motion to adjourn cannot be
made: 1. when a member has possession of the
floor; 2. during the progress of voting; 3. when
the previous question has been ordered; 4. when a
previous motion to adjourn has been the next preceding motion, and no substantial business has
intervened.   By "substantial business" is meant
further debate, another motion and its consideration, or any action which changes the environment
of the renewed motion so that it is really a new
one and not the same one.   This provision is
needful, to guard against factious manœuvres on

the part of the minority. It has been decided also that a defeated motion to table is not "substantial business." Whether, in addition to these limitations, there can also intervene, to delay the putting of a motion to adjourn, a question of privilege or of order, is not so certain. It would seem, however, in view of the urgent nature of these questions, that they would be in order even when a motion to adjourn was pending.[1]

With these few limitations, the motion to adjourn is always first in order.

123. **Effect of Adjournment.** A member obtains the floor, in the usual way, and says: "I move that we adjourn," or "that the assembly do now adjourn." The chair says: "A motion to adjourn is made. Those in favor of adjourning will say 'Aye' * * * It is carried, and the club stands adjourned to Tuesday next." The vote can be doubted, like any other.

If the motion to adjourn is lost, the business interrupted is resumed. If it is carried, the business interrupted is taken up again at the next session, at the point where it was left, unless there

---

[1] See Sections 147 and 158 for the further consideration of this point.

is no further session, in which case an adjournment kills the measure under discussion. If there is a regular order of business, and a regular adjournment, any measure interrupted by adjournment, takes its turn at the next session as " unfinished business," and when it comes up, consideration upon it is resumed at the point interrupted.

124. Fixing the Time. In organizations which have a stated time for adjourning, when that time arrives, the chair, interrupting business, says : " The time for adjournment has arrived ; " then, after waiting a moment (to give a chance for a motion " that the time be extended " or for a motion to adjourn) she adds : " the club stands adjourned." If it is desired to continue the session, an independent motion to extend the time (either indefinitely or definitely) is made, put to vote, and acted upon accordingly.

When there is no fixed time, a motion is made " that the club adjourn at —— o'clock," and this takes its place with other independent motions, having no right of precedence.

Associated also with the motion to adjourn, is the motion to fix the time to which to adjourn, or for re-assembling. All organizations should have a stated hour of assembling; they will then have little need of this motion. When used it is debatable and amendable. It is sometimes said to be entitled to precedence over the motion to adjourn, but, being debatable, it is not so entitled. When a motion to adjourn has been made and the time for the next meeting has not been fixed, the chair, whose duty it is to see that matters are properly conducted, will remind the mover that no time has been fixed for the next session, and she will withdraw her motion to make way for one fixing the time for re-assembling, she retaining the right to renew the motion to adjourn afterward. If she refuses to withdraw the motion to adjourn, it must be put to vote, and the assembly, which "is supposed to know what it wants," as Warrington says, will vote it down, unless they desire no further sessions.

The form of this motion is: "I move that when we adjourn, we adjourn to meet on Tuesday next at three o'clock."

125. The Motion to Lay upon the Table. Second in rank comes the motion to lay upon the table. Its use is to delay final action, or to give time for further investigation. It cannot be debated, amended, committed, postponed, repressed, or reconsidered. It yields only to the motion to adjourn and to questions of privilege and order ; once defeated, it can be renewed only under the same conditions as the motion to adjourn : a defeated motion to adjourn not being " substantial business."

126. **Its Effect.** A motion to lay upon the table, lays upon the table both the measure under consideration and all the questions dependent upon it. It cannot be applied to a part of a question, but, whenever made in reference to a part, applies to the whole. If the motion prevails, the whole matter, with its pending amendments and dependent motions, goes to the table, that is, it is laid aside, suspended; and some other business is taken up.

127. **Taking from the Table.** Immediately afterward or at any later time, either at the same or at a future session, the subject may be taken from the table. The motion to take from the table, however, is not a dependent motion. It has no

right of precedence, and takes its chance with other
motions. It is not debatable. Its effect is to resume the subject at the point interrupted. If a
question is tabled, and no motion is afterward made
to take it up, it is killed. A motion which is on
the table at the close of the session (or club-year)
is finally lost.

Illustration. The motion in section 117 being
under consideration, the dependent motions to
commit, to postpone, and for the previous question, are made ; finally Mrs. Allen says : " I move
to lay upon the table." The chair says : " It is
moved to lay the question upon the table. Those
in favor * * * It is carried, and the question of
the club becoming incorporated goes to the table.
What is now the pleasure of the meeting?" [*Other
business is done.*] Mrs. Allen later, *there being no
business* before the meeting, obtains the floor and
says : " I move to take from the table the motion
'that the club take steps to become incorporated.'"
The chair states the motion, and, if it is carried,
says : " The motion is again before us, and the
first question is upon the pending motion for the
previous question." She then proceeds to put to

vote that motion, and, if it is lost, the other dependent motions, to postpone, to commit and to amend,
and finally, unless it has been otherwise disposed
of, the main question.

It is advisable for the chair, in putting to vote a
motion to lay upon the table, to warn the members
that this motion carries to the table, not only the
main question, but also all the dependent motions
which are attached to it.

SUMMARY

The motion to adjourn takes precedence of all
other motions. When an independent motion, it
may be briefly debated; when dependent, no action
can be taken except to vote upon it.

A motion to adjourn is always first in order, but
it cannot be made, 1. When a member has possession of the floor; 2. During voting; 3. After the
previous question is ordered. 4. When a previous
motion to adjourn immediately precedes it, with no
substantial business intervening. Questions of
privilege and of order may delay the putting of the
motion to adjourn.

A rejected motion to table is not " substantial
business."

If a dependent motion to adjourn is carried, at the next session business is resumed at the point interrupted.

If a meeting adjourns at its regular time, any unfinished business takes its place in the order of business for the next session.

When the time for adjournment is fixed, the chair, after waiting for a motion to adjourn, or to extend the time, declares the meeting adjourned.

When there is no fixed time, a motion is made to fix the time to adjourn. This, with the motion to fix the time for re-assembling, is debatable and amendable.

The motion to lay upon the table yields only to the motion to adjourn. It is subject to the same limitations as that motion and is undebatable.

A motion to lay upon the table temporarily tables the whole subject, with all its dependent motions. If made upon a part, it applies to the whole. It is undebatable.

The subject may be taken up again at any future time by an independent motion to take from the table, the question, with all its dependent motions, being resumed at the point interrupted.

CHAPTER XVI

THE MOTIONS TO POSTPONE

To Postpone to a Stated Time; Its Effect; Limitation; To Postpone Indefinitely; Its Effect.

128. To Postpone to a Stated Time. This motion is fourth in the list, being preceded by the motions to adjourn, to table, and for the previous question. When a motion to postpone is pending, if the previous question is ordered upon the main question, the motion to postpone is "cut off," or quashed; not deferred. On the contrary, if the motion to adjourn or to table prevails while the motion to postpone is pending, it is then simply suspended or laid aside, coming up again in company with the main question to which it is attached, whenever that is resumed. The motion to postpone may be debated and amended (as to the hour), but cannot be committed, tabled, repressed, or, of course, postponed. It cannot be reconsidered, unless this is done immediately. Its object is to assign the subject to some specified time, in order to gain fuller consideration. The effect upon it of the previous question is considered in section 61.

129. **Its Effect.** Like the motion to table, this motion suspends action upon the question; but, while that suspends indefinitely, this assigns definitely. When the subject which was postponed comes up again, it is called a "special assignment." A motion to postpone, postpones the *whole subject*. If the motion to postpone is lost, it can be renewed after substantial business intervenes.

If the motion to postpone is carried, the subject postponed is laid aside, being taken charge of by the secretary, until the time comes to which it was postponed. Then, whatever may be doing, it is in order. The chair interrupts other business and calls it up, or, she failing, the secretary or any member may call for it.

Illustration. The same motion being under discussion as in section 117, and motions having been made to amend, and to commit, Mrs. Paine obtains the floor, as in that section, and says: "I move to postpone the consideration of this question for one

week," or, "I move to postpone for one week."
She may make the time more definite still, as,
"one week from to-day at three o'clock," but she
must assign some time, and not move simply "to
postpone." The chair then says : "It is moved to
postpone this question to one week from to-day at
three o'clock. Are you ready for the question upon
postponement ?" This may be discussed, may be
amended by altering the day or hour, and is finally
put to vote in the usual way. If it is carried (instead of lost, as in section 117), the chair says : "It
is carried, and the consideration of the motion regarding the incorporation of our club is postponed
till next Tuesday at three o'clock." When next
Tuesday arrives, other business is done until three
o'clock, and then the president says : "The time
has arrived to which was assigned the consideration
of the question of incorporation. That matter is
now properly before us as a special order."

If it be desired to finish some other business, a
motion may be made "to lay the special assignment
upon the table; " and if this prevails, it is laid
aside, to be taken up again later. But, if the special
assignment is not laid aside (or, when it is again

taken up), the president continues: "The first question is on the motion to commit" (this having been pending when the main question was postponed); she then proceeds to put the motion to commit to vote, and then whatever other motions are necessary for the disposal of the whole measure.

If the chair fails to call up the question at the specified hour, any one may rise and say: "Mrs. President, has not the time arrived for the special assignment?" She may specify it by name also.

If there is no hour assigned, but simply a day, it comes up under the head of "special assignments."

The interrupted business is laid aside without any *motion* to do so. It is simply held in abeyance till the special assignment is disposed of, to be resumed, either after that is settled or at the next meeting (as unfinished business).

130. Limitation. The motion to postpone can be amended only as to the *time.* It cannot be changed into the motion to postpone indefinitely. Neither can a motion be made to postpone to a day when the association will not be in session, since this is equivalent to a motion to postpone indefinitely.

131. To Postpone Indefinitely. This is not, properly speaking, a motion to postpone, but a motion to reject or repress; it postpones or adjourns a question *sine die*. It is used when there is a desire to summarily dispose of the main question. It stands lowest in the order of precedence, being allowable only when no other dependent motion is pending. It may be debated, but it cannot be amended, postponed, committed, or tabled, and if defeated it cannot be renewed upon the same subject. The effect upon it of the previous question is considered in section 61.

132. Its Effect. When this motion prevails, it simply kills the question to which it applies. Its effect is the same as that of a vote taken upon the question itself, and decided in the negative. It is as if the question were put to vote in the opposite from the regular way, as follows: "Those *not* in favor will say 'Aye.'" This gives the advantage of the affirmative vote to the opponents of the measure, instead of to its advocates. This advantage is not great, however, except when members are indifferent to the result. The motion is chiefly useful as a trial of the strength of the opposition. When the opponents are sure of a majority, it is a quick way of killing a measure. Another name for it, and one that defines its effect, is the motion *to repress.*

Illustration. The illustration in section 117 shows the form of making this motion. If Miss Lovell's motion had been carried instead of lost, the chair would have said: "It is a vote, and the question of the incorporation of the club is indefinitely postponed." This ends the matter; though it may be reconsidered. In order to bring it again before the club a new motion must be made the next club-year.

SUMMARY

The motion to postpone is fourth in the order of precedence.

It may be debated, and amended (as to the time).

It is "cut off" by the previous question.

Its effect is to assign to some definite future time the main question with its attachments, which is then called a "special assignment."

The motion to postpone indefinitely is last in the list.

Its effect is to postpone *sine die*, or repress, the main question; it may be debated and reconsidered.

Its use is to try the strength of the opposition, and to kill a measure without waiting for the regular vote.

CHAPTER XVII

THE MOTION TO COMMIT.

COMMITMENT; EFFECT OF THE MOTION TO COMMIT; TO COMMIT WITH INSTRUCTIONS; PART OF A QUESTION; COURTESIES IN APPOINTMENT; THE INDEPENDENT MOTION.

133. Commitment. "To commit" means "to refer to a committee." This motion is used when it is desirable to have a measure put in better shape, or to gain more information concerning it. It stands fifth in the order of precedence, being superior only to the motions to amend and to repress. The effect upon it when the superior dependent motions are moved is the same as that given in section 128 in regard to the kindred motion to postpone, namely, it is cut off by the previous question and deferred by the others. The motion itself may be debated, but can be neither

postponed, repressed, tabled, nor, of course, committed. The *simple* motion "to commit" cannot
be amended ; but a motion to commit with instructions, or a motion indicating the size of the committee, or the manner of its appointment, can be
amended. It may be reconsidered, if it is done at
once ; but after the committee has been formed,
and has, even in the slightest degree, taken up its
work, the motion to commit is not open to reconsideration. If lost, it can be renewed after substantial business has intervened. The effect upon
it of the previous question is considered in section 61.

Allied to the motion to commit is the motion
" to go into committee of the whole." This means
that the whole assembly resolve itself into a committee, for a less formal discussion of the subject
in hand. When it is desired to go into committee
of the whole, a motion is made "that the assembly
do now resolve itself into a committee of the
whole." If this motion is carried, the presiding
officer calls some other member to the chair, and
takes her place on the floor of the house ; the new
chairman calls the committee to order, and consid-

eration of the question committed follows. There is seldom any occasion for committee of the whole in ordinary assemblies. *See Section 139.*

134. **Effect of the Motion to Commit.** When a measure is pending, and a motion is made " to commit," the effect of this motion, if carried, is to refer to some committee the whole measure under consideration. For the time being, it is removed from the assembly and placed in the hands of a committee. It becomes necessary, therefore, to form that committee at once, and to instruct them. They then take the matter in charge, do as they are instructed, and report back to the assembly, at some future time, the measure as revised by them, adding whatever recommendations they may see fit. It follows that if any amendments are pending when the motion to commit is carried, these are considered by the committee and reported upon also, being incorporated in the main question if favored by them, and omitted if not. A pending motion to repress would be cut off by commitment; there could be no other dependent motions pending, since the other four, if made, would have been decided before the motion to commit.

Illustration. The motion regarding incorporation being under consideration [*see section 117*], Miss Long obtains the floor and says : " I move to commit," or, "to refer the matter to a committee." The chair says : " It is moved to commit. Are you ready for the question ? * * * Those in favor * * * It is carried, and the question whether the club shall become incorporated is referred to a committee. Of how many shall that committee consist ? "

Mrs. Robbins says : "I move that it consist of five." This is discussed, if other numbers are suggested the number is decided upon as shown in section 108 and is settled by vote. The chair then says: "How shall that committee be appointed, — by the chair, or from the floor ? " A motion is made " that it be appointed by the chair " or " that it be nominated from the floor ; " and this is put to vote. If it is the former, the chair appoints, either at once, or as soon thereafter as possible, five members to serve as this committee, the one first named acting as chairman until the committee meets and elects its chairman ; or, the chair may appoint one as the chairman. If the motion to nominate from the floor prevails, the process is that described in sections 6 and 15.[1] The committee may then be instructed in any way, or it may be given "full powers." A motion is made, 1. "That the committee be instructed to consult a lawyer in regard to incorporation, and report at the next meeting;" or, 2. "That the committee be given full powers upon the question of incorporation." *See Section 140.*

If a question is to be referred to a standing committee, the proper motion is, "that the question be referred to the committee on ——." If this is carried, the matter goes to that committee. A motion to refer to a standing committee takes precedence of one to refer to a special committee.

Instead of the simple motion "to commit," a more definite motion may be made, as: "that the subject be referred to a committee of five, to be appointed by the chair." This can be put as one motion, but it is better to "divide" it [*see section 41*] into its three distinct parts, putting each one separately. The form of putting this motion and its effect, are the same as in the simple motion to commit, and it is subject to the same rules; it may be debated and amended at each stage.

[1] See Appendix.

**135. The Motion to Commit with Instruc-
tions.** If a motion to commit is made, including
certain instructions to the committee, these instructions cannot be divided from the rest of the
motion, but must be put to vote with the motion
to commit. If it is desired to get rid of the instructions, or to commit without instructions, a
motion is made "to amend by striking out the instructions." For example, a motion "to refer the
subject to a committee of five, to be appointed by
the chair, and to instruct the committee to consult
a lawyer," cannot be divided into its four parts,
but can be divided into: 1. A motion to refer to a
committee, and instruct them to consult a lawyer;
2. That the number be five; 3. That it be appointed
by the chair. The first motion can then be amended
by a motion "that the instructions be stricken out,"
and it will then be the simple motion to commit.
Other instructions may or may not be inserted afterward. Rule.— *The motion to commit with instructions
is not divisible.*

136. Part of a Question. Any intrinsic part
of a subject can be committed, the other portions
continuing to be acted upon while this is in com-

mittee,— final action on the whole being deferred till the part referred is reported back. This will usually happen when mere verbal improvement is wished for.

137. Courtesies in Appointment. An impression prevails that the mover of the motion to form a committee must necessarily be appointed its chairman. This is one of the courtesies "more honored in the breach than the observance," and one which, since it endangers freedom and equality, should fall into disuse. The chair should appoint, or the assembly nominate, those members who, from interest in the matter, or from general ability, are best fitted to serve, appointing, as often as suitable, one or more new members to serve with the more experienced ones. If the mover is one of those best fitted, she will naturally be chosen on the committee, though not necessarily as its chairman. It has already been said that the one nominated first is not necessarily the chairman, except for the purpose of calling the first meeting. It is well to have a committee consist of an uneven number, in order to avoid ties. Persons who are not present are noti-fied of their appointment by the secretary. All members of a committee are notified of the first meeting by the one whose name stands first on the committee.

Having been committed, the subject is closed for the time being, so far as the society is concerned, and other business is taken up. The mode of procedure when the committee makes its report is considered in the next chapter.

138. **The Independent Motion.** Besides the dependent motion, relating to the main question, there may be made, at any time when no motion is pending, a motion to form a committee for any purpose. This is an independent motion, entitled to no precedence, and subject to any action by means of any of the dependent motions. It is itself the main question.

SUMMARY

The motion to commit is a motion to refer to a committee, or to go into committee of the whole, for conference on a stated matter.

It stands fifth in the order of precedence. It is subject to the same restrictions as the motion to postpone.

Its effect is to refer to some committee, standing or special, the whole subject under consideration, for revision or investigation, the committee to report back to the association.

The motion to commit may designate also the number of members and their manner of appointment; in this case it would better be "divided."

If instructions are included in the motion to commit, they cannot be divided from that motion and put separately to vote; but they may be stricken out by amendment.

Part of a measure may be committed.

It is not necessary to appoint or nominate on a committee the one who makes the motion to commit. Persons not present when appointed are notified by the secretary, who should also give the list to the one first appointed and notify her of the duties assigned.

A motion to form a committee for a specified purpose may also be made ; this is an independent motion, unrelated to another, and is made when no other is pending.

CHAPTER XVIII

THE COMMITTEE AND ITS REPORT

NATURE OF THE COMMITTEE; ITS POWERS; THE REPORT; PRESENTATION OF THE REPORT; ITS RECEPTION; THE MINORITY REPORT; ILLUSTRATION OF REPORTING; RECOMMITMENT.

139. Nature of the Committee. A committee is a dependent body, accountable only for what it is instructed to do, and subject to the society which appoints it. Having been appointed, it meets and organizes as described in sections 4, 5, and 9.

A committee meeting is conducted according to general parliamentary usages, but it may dispense with such formalities as rising to speak and sitting in regular order. Matters may be talked over in a conversational manner; but all action is decided by means of motions and votes in the formal way. A correct record is kept by the secretary, or, if there is no secretary, the chairman notes down all the votes taken. Only those persons chosen to serve upon a committee are competent to take part in its deliberations. No officer, not even the president, is a member of any committee unless she is explicitly put upon it. She is not a member *ex officio*, and any attempt on her part to manipulate or advise committees should be resisted. The quorum is a majority.

The committee of the whole is simply a committee meeting of the whole body. The rules binding upon the assembly when in formal session are suspended, debate is unrestricted, the previous question is not allowed, and the informalities common to all committees are permissible. When the conference is over, the committee of the whole " rises," instead of adjourning, the regular presiding officer resumes the chair, and again calls the assembly to order, the chairman of the committee formally reports its action to the assembly, and this is then acted upon as if it were the report of a small committee.

140. Its Powers. When a committee is instructed, its powers extend only to what it is instructed to do ; when a measure is committed without instructions, the committee revises the measure as to its form, incorporates in it whatever amendments have been passed, and makes some recommendation in regard to it, in a form suitable to be discussed and voted upon by the association. A committee should be careful not to exceed its powers. It can consider only what is referred to it.

When a committee is given " full powers," it is empowered to act as if it were an independent body. A committee is given full powers when something is to be accomplished, which the society has voted to do and can trust to the committee to finish, or, when the decision of a moot question can be left to such committee. Its action is final.

Illustrations. The motion " that the club take steps to become incorporated," being under discussion, a simple motion " to commit " is carried. A committee is appointed forthwith, and the motion is referred to it. The committee considers the feasibility of incorporation, and ascertains what is necessary to be done. At the proper time, it reports, through its chairman, " that the club ought (or ought not) to become incorporated," giving the reasons, and the process necessary.

If, instead, a motion had been made " to refer to a committee with instructions to consult a lawyer," the committee consults a lawyer and reports what he says, making a recommendation, or not, as seems best.

If the motion had been " to refer the matter of incorporation to a committee with ' full powers,' " this would mean that the committee should proceed to get the club incorporated, and, after it had been done, to report to that effect ; or, if after investigation, it disapprove of incorporation, to report " that incorporation of the club is inexpedient." If the club prefers, it can first vote to become incorporated, and then form a committee with "full powers." Such a committee would then proceed to get the club incorporated.

141. **The Report.** When the work of the committee is done, its chairman (or some member instructed to do it) prepares a report which covers all the points referred, with the committee's conclusions concerning them. If the members disagree, the minority may prepare another report (called a " minority report "), embodying their conclusions. Reports are couched in simple, concise language, and if necessary close with some recommendation. For example : a committee instructed " to ascertain the price and desirability of the halls and vestries

in town," will prepare its report somewhat as follows: " Your committee finds the prices of the various halls and vestries to be as follows : Universalist vestry, $2.00 for an afternoon ; Methodist vestry, $3.00 ; Pythian Hall, $1.50 " and so on ; then continuing : " we respectfully suggest that the two places first named seem, for the price, the most desirable. Respectfully submitted, Julia E. Carter, *for the Committee.*"

Again, a committee to whom was referred a proposition without instructions, would report : " Your committee recommend the passage of the measure in the following form " etc., or, "recommend that the measure ought not to be adopted " (giving the reasons), and close in the same way as above.

When given full powers it will report: " Your committee has done the duty assigned to it, and the Methodist vestry is secured as our place of meeting."

142. Presentation of the Report. A committee may, or may not, be instructed to report on a specified day. If it is so instructed, when the day comes, the chair will call for the report, when she comes, in the order of business, to " reports of committees." If not so instructed, when the committee is ready, the one appointed to report will obtain the floor, at some time when no other business is pending, or when reports of committees are called for, and say : " Mrs. President, your committee upon —— is ready to report." The chair will then say: " Shall the report of the committee on —— be now received ? Those in favor * * *" If decided in the negative, the committee must wait till some later time, when the floor must be again obtained and the same procedure followed. If decided in the affirmative, as it usually will be, the committee's representative says : " The committee to whom was referred the question of —— respectfully reports as follows." She will then read her report.

After the report is read, the committee's work is done. There need be no vote to discharge the committee ; it expires with the presentation of its report, and its members have in future no more to do with the matter than any other members, unless they are again instructed to do something further, in which case they are virtually another committee.

143. Reception of the Report. The committee having made its report, that report, which should be in writing, is handed to the presiding officer, and the matter in its new form is then before the meeting for action.

If a motion is then made that the "report be accepted," and this motion is carried, the report, *with its recommendations*, whatever these may be, becomes thereby adopted,[1] and the matter finally closed, such a vote being equivalent to a vote by the assembly itself, upon the whole measure reported, and being decisive of that measure. A vote, therefore, that the report be "accepted" should not be taken except when no discussion and no other action is desired upon the subject, except a simple vote adopting the committee's acts as the acts of the assembly. The presentation of the report is equivalent to a motion to adopt it, and such motion is therefore unnecessary. But if a motion "to adopt" *is* made (simply as a formality) it must not be voted upon until all action is taken upon the report that the assembly wishes. See Reed's Rules, page 81.

---

[1] Accepting the report of a nominating committee does not, of course, elect the officers! It merely accepts the names *as nominees*. And as these must be "accepted" perforce. it is seen that to move "to accept" a nominating committee's report is superfluous.

When the report is simply a report upon some measure, revising it for fresh discussion or presenting new facts for the consideration of the assembly, — *when it is not final,* — a motion "that the report be accepted" is therefore not necessary or best, and it will, if carried, cut off all further consideration. Being in order, the report comes before the meeting without any vote to "adopt" it. Such motion is best made *after* consideration.

A motion may be made "to receive" a report simply as a formality, but this is not necessary; the report having been made, and being in order, is perforce "received," and the only time when this motion is proper is in such cases as the one cited in section 142. A motion "that the report be accepted and adopted" is tautological, either term being sufficient alone, and meaning: *that the assembly adopt, without further discussion, the recommendations or acts of the committee.* Such action is final.

If the time has come for the presentation of a report, and the chair or the committee fails to present it, a member may move "that the report of the committee on —— be now received," or "that it be called for." If this prevails, the committee must report, or explain why they do not. If they are not ready, they may ask for further time, and a motion may be made "that the committee be granted further time and instructed to report on (*naming some day*)." If they wish to be discharged, a vote is taken upon a motion "that the committee be discharged from the consideration of the question of ———." It then comes before the assembly in its original form, and any action may be taken upon it.

144. **The Minority Report**. This report, being simply the dissent of the minority, is not a report, properly speaking. It is read, after the report, as a matter of courtesy, but no action need be taken upon it. It is not before the meeting for consideration. The only thing that can be done with the minority report is to substitute it for the report of the majority. This is the same as an amendment to the report, and it is entitled to no precedence over other amendments.

145. **Illustration of Reporting**. The question of the incorporation of the club having been

referred to a special committee, that committee meets and prepares its report. The club being in session, and the item " reports of committees " having been reached, the chair says : " Are there any committees to report to-day ? "

Mrs. Carter. Mrs. President, your committee on incorporation is ready to report.

The Chair. If there is no objection, the report will be now received. *Or :* We will listen to the report of the committee on incorporation, instructed to report at this time.

Mrs. Carter (reading). Your committee to whom was referred the question of the incorporation of our club, respectfully reports that the proceedings necessary, although a little complicated, can easily be undertaken under the guidance of a friendly gentleman who understands the matter ; we therefore recommend, in view of the advantages of incorporation (which have been forcibly stated by the members, and therefore need not be repeated), that the club take steps at once to become a corporate body.

Respectfully submitted.

JULIA E. CARTER, *for the Committee.*

The Chair (receiving the report from Mrs. Carter), You hear the report of your committee and its recommendation. The matter is now before you, the question recurring upon the motion, now favorably recommended by the committee, " that the club take steps to become incorporated." What is your pleasure? [1] Debate is then in order upon the question whether the club shall become incorporated, and any other action may follow.

It is better for the chair *not* to say : "You have heard the report; what will you do with it?" *Having been made, the report is properly before the meeting*, and the question is open for debate.

146. Recommitment. If the report of a committee is not satisfactory to the assembly, or if, after fresh discussion, new questions arise, the measure may be recommitted, either to the same or to another committee. The motion "to recommit" is subject to the same rules as the motion to commit.

---

[1] The chair may say instead : " You have heard the report of your committee. The matter of incorporation is now before you, and the chair awaits any motion." A motion could then be made " that the club become incorporated," and this would be the basis for action.

SUMMARY

A committee is a dependent body, whose acts are not final; it may dispense with certain formalities, but must decide matters by motion and vote; its members are those who are appointed by the chair, or nominated from the floor, to serve upon it, and none others.   It·considers only what is referred to it.

The committee of the whole, being an informal conference of the assembly as a whole, is released from the formalities of the assembly, and subject to the same rules as any committee.

The powers of the committee extend (1) to what it is instructed to do; (2) to revision of the form of the measure and investigation of facts concerning it; or (3) (in case it is given " full powers "), to carry out the work assigned to it as if it were an independent body, and to report results, which are final.

A written report of what has been done, made as concise as may be, is prepared by some member so instructed in committee.   This is usually followed by some recommendation.

The report is presented when, in the order of

business, the item "reports of committees" is reached, or, at any time when ready, it may report by obtaining the floor for that purpose. It may also be instructed to report at a specified time.

Having reported, the committee's work is done, and it is tacitly discharged, no vote to discharge it being necessary.

A motion "that the report be accepted" is necessary only when such report is one which is final and is not to be considered by the association. A vote "to accept," adopts all the recommendations of the committee without further discussion, and closes the matter.

A motion "to receive" the report is not necessary (except when leave is asked to report out of the proper time), because, having reported, the report is necessarily "received," and is before the assembly for consideration without the formality of a vote to receive.

In case of a report by the minority, this is not properly before the meeting, and can be brought before it only by a motion to amend by substitution.

A measure once committed may be recommitted, either to the same or to a new committee.

Any documents referred to a committee should not be altered or interlined.

Reports of committees, and any other *official* papers, belong to the society and are to be preserved by it.   But a paper or lecture given before a meeting, either by a member or a non-member, belongs to the writer, unless she gives to the society the right to hold, print, or otherwise dispose of it. In absence of a rule to the contrary, all papers are to be kept by the corresponding secretary.

PART V

QUESTIONS OF PRIVILEGE AND ORDER

CHAPTER XIX

QUESTIONS OF PRIVILEGE

NATURE OF THESE QUESTIONS; QUESTION OF PRIV-
ILEGE DEFINED; ITS EFFECT; ILLUSTRATIONS.

147. Nature of these Questions. It has been
pointed out in chapter five, that the regular action
of an assembly is properly carried on by means of
motions. It will sometimes happen, however, that
something occurs requiring immediate action, and
which cannot wait until a new motion would be in
order. A rule is broken, a mistake is made, or an
urgency arises. These must be met; and the means
for meeting them are called questions of privilege
and questions of order. *These are not motions;*
they take precedence of all motions, are always in
order, may interrupt any business (even to taking
the floor from a member), and are decided, temporarily at least, before the pending business is resumed. When they are settled, the business is taken
up again at the point interrupted. A question of

privilege is superior to a question of order, in the line of precedence.

In section 122, it was queried whether among the limitations to the rule that "a motion to adjourn is always first in order," might not also be reckoned the raising of questions of privilege and of order, the claim being that their urgency gives them the right of precedence over even this imperative motion.

Since these questions, if not raised immediately, are not admissible at all, it would seem only right to admit them when a motion to adjourn is pending, as well as when any other motion is pending. A question of privilege, if not really urgent, could be ruled inadmissible by the chair after it was stated by the member, and this would dispose of the difficulty so far as that is concerned; while in regard to the question of order, inasmuch as, to be admissible, *it must relate to the matter pending* (see sections 151 and 153), it could never interrupt a motion to adjourn except in a case where the mover of that motion, in making it, broke one of the four rules given in section 122, and the question of order were raised to correct her error. The further provision, that *if a motion to adjourn be interrupted, the question interrupting it must be decided without debate or appeal,* would seem to guard sufficiently the "right of the assembly to terminate its sitting at any time," which rule is the reason for the high rank of the motion to adjourn. The conclusion is therefore, that, in spite of the rigidity of the rule that the "motion to adjourn is always first in order," a question of privilege or of order, in the rare cases where it could occur, would interrupt such motion, taking precedence of the motion to adjourn as well as of all other motions. See page 220 for an illustration.

148. Questions of Privilege Defined. Questions of privilege are questions relating to some matter foreign to the business in hand; they usually raise some query regarding the rights and privileges of the assembly itself, or of some individual member thereof. They rarely occur, and they can be easily settled. A good example arose a number of years ago in the United States Senate, when it was suspected that newspaper reporters were secreted in the Senate galleries during the secret sessions. They had no right there, these sessions not being open to the public, and by their

presence the privilege of the Senate to hold sessions closed to the public was abridged. A senator
raised a question of privilege, and means were
taken to expel the intruders. Other examples
would be: the sudden extinction of the lights; the
need of ventilation; the disturbance of a meeting
by a disorderly member or outsider; the desire of a
member to make an immediate statement or report,
rendered obligatory because of her sudden and
necessary departure; an injustice done to a member; charges against official character in a misre-
ported speech; in short, any exigency which
imperatively requires attention. Rising to make
an explanation is not necessarily a question of privilege. A member is usually allowed, as a matter of
courtesy, to take the floor for an explanation, but
has no right to it; if there is objection, the question of granting time to make an explanation is put
to vote and decided by the majority. It cannot
interrupt other business.

149. **Its Effect**. It is the prerogative of the
chair to decide whether a question thus interjected
is, or is not, properly a question of privilege. The
member who wishes to raise it, does not obtain the

floor as in making a motion, but rises, interrupts business, if necessary, and says: "Mrs. President, I rise to a question of privilege." She is asked by the chair to state it, does so, the chair decides whether it is a proper question of privilege, and if she says it is not, the member may appeal. If it is allowed, a motion [1] is then made, in order to bring the matter before the assembly for discussion ; and this motion is considered at once, though not of necessity *decided* at once, since it may be tabled, postponed, — in short, treated like any other motion. All proceedings are stayed till it is decided; then they are resumed, a member interrupted retaining her right to the floor.

150. Illustrations. A certain measure is under discussion, and Mrs. Paine is speaking.

Mrs. Friend (interrupting). Mrs. President, I rise to a question of privilege.

The Chair (rising). The member will state her question of privilege. [*Mrs. Paine sits.*]

Mrs. Friend. I am very sorry to say it, Mrs. President, but it is impossible for those of us who

---

[1] Or, in certain cases, by the chair's request the matter is adjusted without a motion and vote.

are seated in the rear of the hall to hear what is said, on account of the whispering of certain members. (*Sits.*)

The Chair. This must certainly be regarded as a proper question of privilege, the first right of the club being its right to hear what is said. If we all would speak freely what we have to say, *on our feet*, this trouble need never occur. The chair will ask the members to preserve order and quiet. Mrs. Paine will proceed.

(*Mrs. Paine rises and goes on with her remarks.*)

Mrs. Allen. Mrs. President, I rise to a question of privilege.

The Chair. You will state it, please.

Mrs. Allen. There is a very violent knocking somewhere (almost as distracting as the knocking in Macbeth). Cannot the doorkeeper, or some one, be asked to investigate?

The Chair. The chair will entertain any motion upon this question of privilege.

Mrs. Allen. I move that the doorkeeper be invited to ascertain the cause of this disturbance.

[*This is put to vote ; the doorkeeper does as she is instructed, returns and reports the trouble (unless she*

has adjusted it herself), *and whatever action is necessary follows, business being suspended meanwhile.*]

* * * * * *

Miss Long. Mrs. President, I rise to a question
of privilege.

The Chair. Miss Long will state *her* question.

Miss Long. I am obliged to go now, and have
been waiting in vain for a chance to ask for some
instruction in regard to the work of our committee
on the library. The matter cannot very well wait.

The Chair. The question is properly raised.
What is the pleasure of the meeting?

Miss Lovell. I move that Miss Long have time
to make her statement.

[*This is put to vote, and action follows accordingly,
the business in hand being interrupted, and then resumed after this question is decided.*]

SUMMARY

Questions of privilege and of order are not motions; they take precedence of all motions, may
interrupt any business, and are always in order.

A question of privilege takes precedence of a
question of order.

It relates to something foreign to the business in hand, and raises some question regarding the rights or privileges of the assembly or of its members.

Its effect is to stay all proceedings till it is decided. The chair decides whether the question is a proper question of privilege; a motion and vote follow, unless the matter can be adjusted by request of the chair.

CHAPTER XX

QUESTIONS OF ORDER

Definition ; Duty of the Chair ; Effect of this Question ; The Appeal ; Tie Vote on the Appeal ; Limitations ; Precedence ; Illustrations.

151. **Definition.** A question of order differs from a question of privilege in being *directly related to the matter in hand*, and in tending to correct or perfect the proceedings regarding it. Speaking not to the question ; making a motion when it is not in order of precedence ; indulging in personalities ; breaking any parliamentary rule, are examples ; the

chair may be out of order (for entertaining a motion not admissible, or for refusing to put one that is, for instance) — and all these breaches are occasions for raising a "question of order," which is also often called a "point of order." It takes precedence of everything except a question of privilege.

152. Duty of the Chair. It is the first duty of the chairman to preserve order and decorum ; and this means, to preserve not only an orderly demeanor of the assembly as a whole, but also to call to order any member who commits a breach of order or a serious parliamentary error. If the chair fails to notice any such occurrence, a question of order is raised by any member.

153. Effect of a Question of Order. When the question of order is raised, all business pending is interrupted, is suspended till the point is settled, and then is resumed. If a member is speaking, she retains the right to the floor, after the question of order is settled, unless she herself is decided to have been out of order. In this case, if objection is made, she cannot proceed, even if in order, without a vote allowing her so to do.

The course of proceeding is similar to that of the question of privilege. When the occasion arises, the member, without regularly obtaining the floor, rises and says : " Mrs. President, I rise to a question of order." She is asked by the chair to state it; she does so, and the chair then decides whether it is " well taken," saying : " The chair decides the question of order to be well taken," or " to be not well taken." This declaration of the chair, which is called a " ruling," decides the question (subject to appeal), and matters proceed in accordance with her ruling. There is no vote taken, and no submission of the question to the assembly for discussion. It is thus seen to be very different from a motion.[1]

Since it must relate directly to the business in hand, it follows that a point of order must be raised immediately upon the occasion for it; if it is delayed, and other business intervenes, it cannot be raised at all. If it relates to words spoken in debate, these words are taken down by the secretary when the objection to them is raised.

---

[1] The chair may allow remarks before giving her ruling, but she is not obliged to; and she may stop them and give her decision at any time.

154. The Appeal. If any member is dissatisfied with the ruling of the chair, she may "appeal,"
by rising and saying : " I appeal from the decision
of the chair." The chair may, but need not, insist
upon a second to an appeal, which is made by some
other member rising and saying : " I second the
appeal." .The question is now removed from the
control of the chair, and is decided by the assembly, which by vote overrules or sustains the chair's
ruling, the majority deciding it. The form for putting this question is : " Shall the decision of the
chair stand as the judgment (or decision) of the
meeting ? " Debate follows, — in which the chairman may take precedence over other members,
giving her reasons for her ruling, without leaving
the chair, — and then the question is put to vote,
and declared as follows : " The decision of the
chair is sustained," or " overruled," as the case
may be. This vote decides the matter finally ; it
cannot be reconsidered. It is thus seen, that in
this, as in all other matters, *final* authority rests
with the whole body, and not with the chairman.
As Warrington says : " The right of appeal is in-
dispensable to the free action of all assemblies,

the presiding officer not being the master, but the servant."

155. Tie Vote on an Appeal. A tie vote on a *motion* defeats the motion, as has been shown. A tie vote upon an appeal has the opposite effect; it affirms, instead of defeating. The decision of the chair is sustained thereby. The reason for this is that the ruling of the chair is assumed to stand, unless it is overthrown; and since a tie vote "accomplishes nothing," it cannot overrule a decision. The chair will then not need (as she would not wish) to vote to sustain her own decision. Rule: *The effect of a tie vote on an appeal is to decide affirmatively the question: "Shall the decision of the chair stand?"*

156. Limitations. A question of order cannot be committed, amended, or reconsidered. It cannot be tabled or postponed without at the same time tabling or postponing the whole matter out of which the question of order arose. The same is true of the appeal. It cannot be acted upon by any of these motions, separately from the proceedings out of which the question of order arose. If any dependent motion is made while an appeal is pending, it applies to the whole matter under discussion, which is postponed, committed (or, as the case may be), appeal, question of order, and all. A motion to lay upon the table, therefore, lays upon the table the whole subject under consideration.[1] As an appeal is usually debatable, it would seem that, when debatable, the previous question can be applied to it, when *expressly moved upon the appeal. See section 61.*

If a point of order *upon* a point of order is raised, the second is decided first, but, to avoid complications, is not debatable, nor open to appeal. If the question under discussion when the point of order is raised, is undebatable, the appeal is undebatable. If a question of order interrupts a motion to adjourn, it must be decided without debate or appeal. *See section 147.*

157. **Precedence.** It may be well to repeat here the rule regarding the rank of dependent questions: 1. Question of privilege; 2. Question of order; 3. Motion to adjourn; 4. Motion to lay on the table; 5. Call for the previous question; 6. Motion to

---

[1] See the introduction, for the practice of the United States House of Representatives, which, *by special rule*, is the opposite of this.

postpone; 7. Motion to commit; 8. Motion to amend; 9. Motion to postpone indefinitely.

Besides these, there are some other matters which may also be considered when an independent motion is pending. The chief of these are: the withdrawal and division of a motion; raising the question of "no quorum;" motions in regard to the manner of taking the vote, to limit or to extend debate, to fix the time for closing debate, to fix the time for adjourning or for re-assembling; to suspend a rule; to take a recess. Each one of these is in order when the necessity for it arises, and takes precedence of the pending independent motion.

158. Illustrations.— Questions of Order and Appeals. The Mendon Women's Club being in session, and the item "new business" being reached, the following action follows:—

Mrs. Burns. Mrs. President.

The Chair. Mrs. Burns.

Mrs. Burns. I move that at the close of the season, our club have a luncheon. It will be helpful to sociability, and I am sure we should all enjoy it.

The Chair. You hear the motion, that the club

have a luncheon to close its season. The question is before you for discussion.

Miss Lovell. Mrs. President.

The Chair. Miss Lovell.

Miss Lovell. Why could we not call it a break-fast instead? I move to amend by striking out the word "luncheon," and inserting the word "break-fast."

The Chair. You have heard —

Mrs. Burns. Mrs. President, I accept the suggestion. It makes no difference what we *call* it, so that we have it.

The Chair. The amendment is accepted, and the question is now upon having a *breakfast* to close our club season.

Mrs. Allen. Mrs. President.

The Chair. Mrs. Allen.

Mrs. Allen. I object to this motion. There will be a great deal of expense attendant upon it, and I am sure many of us could not afford it. Do let us have *one* society in town that leaves *eating* out of its programme! There is the Young Women's Club, and the J. R. S. and the K. C. L.! They are always having suppers; and I'm sure why they wish —

The Chair (*rising*). The member will kindly proceed in order. She is at present speaking off the question. Criticism of other clubs is not in order.

Mrs. Allen. Very well; I will endeavor to proceed in order, Mrs. President. I am decidedly opposed to this idea!

Miss Sawyer. Mrs. President.

The Chair. Miss Sawyer.

Miss Sawyer. I am as decidedly in favor of it. We need something of a social nature in order to cement our club friendship and make us a little family, as it were. Breaking bread together always helps the spirit of good fellowship without which no club can be a success.

Mrs. Preston. Mrs. President.

The Chair. Mrs. Preston.

Mrs. Preston. I move to lay this question upon the table. I, for one, think —

The Chair. The motion to table is undebatable, and the member is therefore out of order. Are you ready for the question?

Mrs. Paine. Mrs. President, I rise to a question of order.

The Chair. You will please state it.

Mrs. Paine. The chair, after stating that the motion to table is undebatable, asks us if we are ready for the question, thereby implying that debate is invited.

The Chair. The point shows that our member is wide-awake, but it is not well taken nevertheless. The chair asked: "Are you ready?" to give opportunity for a possible motion to adjourn or for a new point of order — those taking precedence of the motion to table. Are you ready? Those in favor of the motion to lay this motion on the table will say "Aye" * * * It is lost.

Mrs. Robbins. Mrs. President.

The Chair. Mrs. Robbins.

Mrs. Robbins. I move to postpone its consideration for one week.

The Chair. It is moved to postpone for one week. Are you ready?

Miss Long. Mrs. President.

The Chair. Miss Long.

Miss Long. I move to refer the matter to a committee consisting of —

Mrs. Robbins. Mrs. President, I rise to a question of order. The motion to commit is not now in order, a motion to postpone being pending.

The Chair. The point is well taken. The motion to commit is not now in order, the motion to postpone taking precedence. Are you ready to vote on the motion to postpone? Those in favor * * * It is lost.

Miss Long. Mrs. President.

The Chair. Miss Long.

Miss Long. I now renew my motion to refer it to a committee consisting of the president, treasurer, and recording secretary.

The Chair. You hear the motion. The chair will divide the motion, putting first the motion to commit. Are you ready?

Miss Faxon (remaining seated). *I* think we ought to dispose of this matter in the club itself.

Mrs. Young. Mrs. President, I rise to a question of order.

The Chair. Mrs. Young will please state her question.

Mrs. Young. The last speaker did not rise and address the chair.

The Chair. The chair decides that point to be well taken. All debate must be regularly proceeded with.

Miss Faxon (*rising*). I stand corrected, Mrs. Chairman, and am opposed to the committee, because it gives too much power to a few.

The Chair. The assembly could of course instruct its committee after appointment. Are you ready?

Mrs. Robbins
Mrs. Paine } (*rising at once*). Mrs. President.

The Chair. Mrs. Robbins.

Mrs. Robbins. I move —

Mrs. Carter. I rise to a point of order.

The Chair. State your point of order, please.

Mrs. Carter. Mrs. Paine rose before Mrs. Robbins, Mrs. President. She is seated so far from the chair, that probably the chair overlooked her. Is she not entitled to the floor rather than Mrs. Robbins?

The Chair. The chair must decide that point to be not well taken. She saw both members rise, and gives the floor to Mrs. Robbins; unless Mrs. Robbins yields (?).

Mrs. Robbins. Since I am entitled to the floor, I think I'll keep it, Mrs. President. I move —

Mrs. Carter. I appeal from the decision of the chair.

The Chair. Mrs. Carter appeals from the chair's decision. The question is, Shall the decision of the chair stand as the judgment of the club? [*Debate may follow.*] Those in favor of sustaining the chair will say "Aye" * * * It is a vote; the decision of the chair is affirmed, and Mrs. Robbins will resume, the question being upon the motion to commit.

Mrs. Robbins. I move the club do now adjourn.

The Chair. A motion to adjourn is made. Those in favor * * * It is lost. Those in favor of the motion to commit * * * It is lost. What is the further pleasure of the club?

Mrs. Ellis. It looks to me, Mrs. President, as if certain members of this club think more of defeating a motion they don't like, than of getting a fair debate upon it. One speaker here has left no stone unturned to secure her object!

Mrs. James. I rise to a question of order.

The Chair. Please state it.

Mrs. James. The last speaker is indulging in *decided* personalities.

The Chair. The point of order is well taken. Mrs. Ellis will confine herself to the question.

Mrs. Ellis. I appeal from your ruling, Mrs. President. I have been careful to use no names, and I think I am strictly in order.

The Chair. An appeal is taken. Shall the decision of the chair stand? Those in favor * * * It is lost. Mrs. Ellis is decided to be in order, and may proceed.

Mrs. Ellis. I only desire a fair discussion of a very important question, and I think—

Miss Willis. Mrs. President.

The Chair. Miss Willis.

Miss Willis. I move we adjourn.

The Chair. A motion is made to—

Mrs. Paine. Mrs. President, I rise to a question of order.

The Chair. Please state it.

Mrs. Paine. The floor cannot be taken from a member for the making of a motion to adjourn.

The Chair. The chair decides the point to be well taken, and the motion to adjourn to be out of order. Mrs. Ellis will resume.

Mrs. Ellis. I therefore move to postpone the whole matter to two weeks from to-day.

Mrs. Granger. Mrs. President, I rise to a question of order.   Have we not already voted not to postpone?   Is a second motion in order?

The Chair.   New business having intervened, a second motion to postpone is in order.   Are you ready?   Those in favor * * * It is carried, and the question of holding a breakfast is postponed, and will be made a special assignment for two weeks from to-day.   The chair hopes the members will take special pains to be present on that occasion, so that there may be no lack of due consideration.   The time has now come to adjourn —

Mrs. Friend.   I move we adjourn.

The Chair.   Those in favor will say " Aye," * * * The club stands adjourned to one week from to-day at 2.30 o'clock.

SUMMARY

A question (or point) of order relates to the matter in hand, and tends to perfect or correct it.

It is the duty of the chair to preserve order and correct parliamentary errors.   If she fails, a member " raises a question of order."

The effect of this question is to suspend proceedings till it is decided.

The member raising it does not "obtain the floor," but interrupts business anywhere and at any time.

It must be raised immediately upon the occasion for it; if business intervenes, it is inadmissible.

The chair decides whether the point is, or is not, "well taken;" and this settles the matter, subject to appeal.

Any one dissatisfied with the ruling may appeal. The question whether the ruling shall stand is then decided by a majority vote.

A tie vote upon an appeal affirms the chair's decision.

Neither a question of order, nor an appeal from the decision upon it, can be committed, amended, or reconsidered; the question and also the appeal can neither be tabled nor postponed, without at the same time tabling or postponing the whole subject to which they relate. When the appeal is debatable, as it usually is, the previous question may be moved upon it.

CONCLUSION

THE principles and forms given in tne foregoing chapters are to be used as a guide in conducting meetings. Reading, or even study, however, is not enough to fit one to become a good parliamentarian. For this, *practice* is necessary; and societies that wish to conduct their sessions properly are recommended to hold occasional or regular executive sessions, at which parliamentary law may be practised. These sessions can be mock sessions simply for practice; but it is more helpful to adopt the custom of doing the regular business of the society in periodical executive sessions of the whole membership, thereby practising and accomplishing something besides. A club whose business is done by a small directors' board, or committee, has no opportunity for this general practice. By holding an occasional executive meeting (taking one of the regular club days for it), by bringing up before it matters of business, and by discussing, modifying, and taking final action upon them, the members will learn more in one year than they could in five by mere study and play-practice. The text-book can be used for study at home and for reference at the club. In addition to this, those members specially interested could meet occasionally and read and practise together. These methods have been pursued with great profit in several associations known to the author; and those societies in which opportunity is given for *all* to have a voice and a vote in the business, are conspicuously progressive, wide-awake, and able to "agree to disagree."

An organization wishing to adopt this manual as its guide, will insert in its by-laws a section similar to this: The meetings of this club shall be conducted by the rules of parliamentary procedure, the "Woman's Manual of Parliamentary Law" being the authority. This manual is then its final authority.

If any society may wish to dissent from some procedure recommended by its authority, a special rule can be made, setting forth the procedure the society prefers, and such special rule will govern that society in that instance, instead of the rule laid down in the manual. This special rule need not be included in the by-laws; a recorded vote is equally binding. For example, a certain society having adopted the "Woman's Manual," may deem it advisable that all motions *shall* be seconded, or, that the making of the motion to reconsider shall not be restricted. A rule may then be adopted "that in this club every motion shall be seconded before it is stated," or, "that in this club the motion to reconsider may be made by any member." Of course, no society will make a special rule offsetting those usages which are universally recognized, if they desire to be parliamentary at all; but, having adopted its authority, a society may then make its own special rules authorizing such other procedure in certain cases as it may prefer.

Its manual will then be its authority in all matters upon which it has made no special rules; while any special rules which it has adopted will be superior, upon the special matters to which they relate, to its parliamentary authority. A society may adopt special rules upon any matter affecting its work or methods, these to be included in its by-laws or, better, adopted separately as "special rules," or "regulations." Care however should be taken not to adopt a special rule which conflicts with an established principle (i.e., a principle upon which there is no conflict of authorities) ; *should* such a rule be adopted, it must be strictly construed. *See appendix to section 15.*

It might well be added here that a club should be careful not to establish any precedent (from any false ideas of courtesy or any other reason) which will restrict its freedom in any way, and especially in its choice of officers. Should some such bad precedent have become established, the sooner it is disregarded the better. Precedents are not like "the laws of the Medes and Persians;" they are binding only until a better practice supervenes.

Finally, if a society finds that something has been done incorrectly in the past, it is best to let such past procedure remain as it is ; not to try to go back and correct it, but to do it correctly the *next time.* No one having objected at the time, it is to be assumed that matters were rightly managed, and the action thus taken will stand.

FINAL SUMMARY

Parliamentary Law is not fixed nor arbitrary, but is in process of development.

Such usages as have become generally adopted are properly a part of parliamentary law.

No one manual, or authority, is final.

Each society votes to adopt that authority which it likes best. Having adopted an authority, it must follow the rules which such authority lays down. *Provided*, that any society may make any special rule, offsetting any procedure recommended by its accepted authority, this special rule of its own then governing instead of the book.

Where there is a conflict of authorities, that one which seems best fitted to the needs of the society in question should be accepted and indorsed.

Fairness, expediency, and reasonableness are the basic principles to apply in deciding the usefulness of a given procedure.

The chief leading principles upon which parliamentary law is founded may be said to be: 1. justice, 2. equality, 3. order, 4. speed (doing the work as rapidly as is consistent with fairness and accuracy), 5. the right of the majority to decide (which is secured by the vote), and 6. the right of the minority to be heard (which is secured by the debate). In passing a vote, adopting a rule or framing a constitution, these fundamental principles should be subserved so far as possible. A society *may*, however, make a rule conflicting with any of these principles, which rule will then supersede the principle; but in such cases, the rule extends only so far as it explicitly states.

Motions that cannot be debated: the dependent motion to adjourn, motions to lay upon and to take from the table, to suspend a rule, to limit and to extend debate, to decide upon the manner of taking the vote, to reconsider an undebatable motion, and, in general, any matter that interrupts an undebatable motion.

Motions that cannot be amended: to adjourn, to lay upon and to take from the table, for the previous question, to indefinitely postpone, to suspend a rule, to decide upon the manner of taking the vote, and to reconsider.

Motions that cannot be reconsidered: to adjourn, to lay upon and to take from the table, for the previous question, to commit (after the committee has taken action), to limit or to extend debate, to suspend a rule, and to reconsider; also elections to membership or to office.

Matters that require unanimous consent: the secretary casting one ballot for the whole, election by acclamation, voting upon names collectively, suspension of rules, expunging from the records, withdrawal of a motion, resuming debate after the affirmative is put; also, in general, any irregularity which the meeting seems willing, for the time being, to allow.

Suspension of Rules: By "rules" is meant, properly speaking, any special regulation concerning details of work. Some rules, so-called, are really more properly called by-laws. For examples of rules *see sections 47, 55, 57, 69, 74, 80, 81, 119.* The term "rules" does not include the constitution, and could include only such by-laws as are capable of temporary suspension. For instance, the by-law prescribing the time of meeting could be suspended, but not the one fixing the fee. A parliamentary principle or an item in the parliamentary authority cannot be "suspended."

APPENDIX

MODEL OF A CONSTITUTION AND BY-LAWS

To be varied to suit the needs of the society in question

CONSTITUTION[1]

ARTICLE I. *Name.*— This club shall be known as the (Mendon Women's Literary Club).

ARTICLE II. *Object.* — Its object shall be (the mutual improvement of its members in literature, art, science, and the vital interests of the day).

ARTICLE III. *Officers.* — Its officers shall be a president, a vice-president, a recording and a corresponding secretary, a treasurer and an auditor. [*If a Board of Directors is desired, that is provided for here; viz.,* "and a board of (seven) directors."] There shall also be (three) lecture committees of (three) members each. These officers and committees shall be elected by the club at each annual meeting, as provided for in the by-laws. The business of the club shall be transacted by its members,

---

[1] If a club is incorporated, its charter may take the place of its Constitution. The By-laws will then include the matter here given in both instruments.

in executive meetings held once a month. [*If there are directors, this last sentence will be omitted.*]

ARTICLE IV. *Meetings.* — The club shall hold an annual business meeting on the (fourth Tuesday in March) and an afternoon meeting every (Tuesday) from (October) to (March) inclusive. The (third Tuesday) of every month from (October) to (February) inclusive shall be a business meeting of members, and all important business shall be finally voted upon at these business meetings only. None but members shall be present, except as provided in the by-laws. (Seven) members shall constitute a quorum. Members shall be notified of regular meetings by an (announcement in the Mendon *Telegraph*). Special meetings may be called by the president, upon the written application of any (five) members, all members to be specially notified of the proposed meeting.

ARTICLE V. *Financial Year.* — The financial year shall begin on the (first Tuesday in October), and the fee then payable from each member shall be (two dollars). If the fee is not paid before the expiration of one (month) from the time of election, or from the beginning of the financial year, the person from whom it is due, having been notified, shall cease to be a member.

ARTICLE VI. *Membership.*— Any (two) members
(of one year's standing) may present, in writing, at
any regular meeting, the name of any woman wishing to become a member. The name shall then lie
upon the table till the meeting (one) week later,
announcement being made of such application. [*If
it is desired to restrict membership in any way, such
restriction is added here.*] Each name shall be voted
on separately, by ballot [*white and black balls may
be used, or blank slips of paper on which are written
" Yes " or " No "*], and the applicant declared elected
unless (three) negative votes be cast. A candidate
failing of election shall not be eligible again that
club year. The membership shall be limited to
(100).

BY-LAWS

ARTICLE I. DUTIES OF OFFICERS.— SECTION 1.
President and Vice-President. — The president shall
preside at all meetings, and conduct them by a
formal order of business, shall deliver an annual
address, and shall perform the other duties usually
belonging to this office. In case of her absence or
disability, these duties shall be performed by the
vice-president, or by the chairmen of the lecture
committees, in their order. The vice-president shall

hold herself ready to assist the president in any way.

SECT. 2. *Secretaries.* — The recording secretary shall keep a correct record of all meetings. The corresponding secretary shall receive, read to the club, and answer, all letters relating to club affairs, and preserve all club papers. She shall notify members of their election, and of the limit of time when their fees are due in order to continue members; shall sign and deliver all tickets of membership, keep a correct list of members with their addresses, and attend to all other business of the club relating to its membership and its docu-' ments. She shall make a written report of the year's transactions and present outlook of the club at the annual meeting. [*This duty may be given to the recording secretary instead.*] The records and correspondence shall be open at all times to the inspection of the club. [*In clubs where there is a great deal of correspondence with other clubs, especially where a club belongs to the "General Federation of Women's Clubs," another secretary may be added, called a Federation Secretary, whose duty will be strictly to attend to the correspondence with other clubs and with the Federation.*]

SECT. 3. *Treasurer.* — The treasurer shall receive, collect, hold, and pay out all club moneys, subject to the order of the club. She shall keep a correct account in detail of all moneys received and expended by her, and shall render her report in writing at the annual meeting.

SECT. 4. *Auditor.* — The auditor shall audit all bills and the accounts of the treasurer, and report, in writing, at the annual meeting whether they are correct.

[*If there are directors, a section defining their duties is added here. There will then be no "business meetings," strictly speaking, as the business will be done by the directors. See section 12; also appendix to these by-laws.*]

SECT. 5. *Lecture Committees.* — The (three) lecture committees shall be called : 1. The Department of (Art and Literature) ; 2. The Department of (Science and Economics) ; 3. The Department of (Ethics and History). The (first and second Tuesdays of October and November) shall be in charge of the first department ; the (first and second Tuesdays of December) in charge of the second department ; and the (first and second Tuesdays of February and March) in charge of the third department. The chairman of each of these committees shall make a written report at the annual meeting of the work done by her committee during the year. The programme for all other meetings shall be arranged by the club at its monthly business meetings.

SECT. 6. *Election.* — At the (business meeting in February), the president shall appoint a committee of three, no member of which shall be an officer or a chairman of a lecture committee, to nominate a list of officers and lecture committees for the ensuing year. This nominating committee shall notify their nominees, and, in case of any refusals, shall supply their places. They shall then present the perfected list to the members at the (third regular meeting in March). At the annual business meeting, the election shall take place, and shall be by ballot; if any person nominated be not elected, the club may ballot till every position is filled. [*Here may be added, if necessary, any other provision to secure a fair election. See Election of Officers, sections 14 to 18.*] (No one shall be eligible to office who has been a member less than one year.)

SECT. 7. *Term of Office.* — No person shall hold more than one official position at any time, nor (with the exception of the secretaries and the treasurer) shall serve for a longer period than (two) successive years in the office to which she may be elected; but any person shall be eligible for re-election after the intervention of (one year) from the time she last held the position. The term of office shall expire with the annual meeting. *See section 29.*

ARTICLE II. *Members.*—Every one who is elected a member, on signing the constitution and paying the fee, shall be entitled to receive a membership ticket, and shall be admitted to all the privileges of the club to the close of the financial year, after which her membership may be continued by the payment of the annual fee. Members must be ready to show their tickets at the door at every meeting.

Honorary members may be elected at the discretion of the club. Members who apply for re-election may, by unanimous consent, be re-elected by acclamation. Former members who live at a distance may become "corresponding members," and, by paying visitor's fees, attend the meetings when in (Mendon). *See appendix to these by-laws.*

Any member who desires to withdraw from the club shall send a written notice of her intention to the corresponding secretary.

ARTICLE III. *Visitors.* — Members may bring friends to any meeting by the payment of (fifteen cents) for each friend. No one visitor, however, shall attend more than one meeting in the same club-year, except non-residents of (Mendon), and the guests of members. Three complimentary tickets shall be given to each lecturer before the club.

ARTICLE IV. *Conduct of Meetings.* — All meetings shall be conducted by the rules of parliamentary law, (the "Woman's Manual of Parliamentary Law") being the authority. No person, except the corresponding secretary, shall print, or cause to be printed, any report of any meeting, unless authorized by vote of the club.

ARTICLE V. *Amendments.* — This constitution and by-laws may be amended at any regular business meeting of the club, by a (two-thirds vote) of the members present and voting, provided that a written notice of the intended change has been given at the meeting at least (one week) previous.[1] *See appendix.*

ARTICLE VI. *Suspension of Rules.* — Any provision in this constitution and by-laws which is capable of being temporarily laid aside may be "suspended," for not more than one meeting, by unanimous consent.

---

[1] Valuable suggestions will be found in Mrs. Olive Thorne Miller's little book entitled, "The Woman's Club. A Practical Guide and Hand Book," published by the United States Book Company, New York.

APPENDIX

To Section 10. — In electing a committee by acclamation, it is better not to vote upon a name as soon as it is nominated, but instead, to receive all the nominations at once, before voting upon any of them (asking for further nominations, as in section 6); and then, all having nominated who wish, to vote upon the names, one by one, in the order nominated, until the requisite number is chosen. This gives the meeting a chance to have all its nominees before it at once, and to reject some in favor of others, if it chooses.

To Section 12. — An extended experience and observation have led the author to think that in large clubs (those, say, whose attendance at business sessions exceeds one hundred) all *details* of business might better be done by a board of directors. Where there is such a board, if its powers are undefined, the association virtually delegates all its rights. If, therefore, the body at large wishes to do any of its work in executive session, provision should be made for such executive sessions, and the powers of its directors should be carefully defined, in its by-laws. These powers must not be exceeded.

To Section 14. — Errors in spelling, abbreviations, initials instead of full names, omission of middle initials and such inadvertences do not invalidate a ballot. Non-members cannot be elected to office. All ballots, except blanks, are to be counted in the "whole number cast," and the tellers should report any name which has received more than one vote.

To Section 15. — The general principle in elections is *the right of independent voting*, that is, the right of the voter to vote

for whomsoever she pleases. This right cannot be set aside
except by the most definite and explicit restrictions, adopted
prior to the balloting. If, for instance, a certain method is
prescribed in the by-laws or by vote, for nominating officers,
this method does not preclude other nominations, unless such
are definitely forbidden; nor does it preclude any voter from
writing in the name of some person not nominated, unless
some vote or by-law says that only those persons shall be candidates whose names are on the one prescribed list — a provision which would be very arbitrary and unwise.

· The question of which is the best method of nominating and
electing officers is a very difficult one. In choosing between
methods the end should be to secure both *fairness* and *secrecy;*
i.e., a secret ballot, and an equal chance for all. This must
be modified also, by a certain amount of regard for forethought
in the selection of candidates. Whatever method will secure
all this is the best one. Of the methods for nomination described in the text, the ordinary nominating committee is the
simplest and most careful, and (especially where there is rotation in office) is open to very little objection. When this
method is supplemented by allowing and encouraging any
number of independent additional nominees, and when the
election is by printed ballot, this method will generally be
satisfactory.

Another very good method is to nominate by what is called
" an informal ballot " and to elect by a formal ballot at the
same or a subsequent meeting.

Informal Ballot for Nominees : — Each voter writes upon a
slip of paper the name she prefers for President. These slips
are collected, and (1) every name offered is considered a nominee; or (2) only the two or three names receiving the *highest
number* of votes, or again, (3) all the names which receive

a *certain number* of votes, are considered nominees. (It is decided beforehand which of these three ways to select the first way being the fairest.) These are the candidates for President. Other officers are then nominated in the same way. The names of all candidates should be clearly announced, or, better, exposed upon a blackboard.

Election by Formal Ballot. — If the election is at the same meeting, the members, having all the nominees before them, proceed to write upon slips, the name they prefer for President, balloting until some one receives a majority vote. They then go on to the other offices. This is the formal ballot and is decisive. If the election is at a subsequent meeting (which is much better) the members will vote by means of printed or written ballots, which have been prepared in the interim; and upon these ballots are inscribed all the names, in alphabetical order, which were regularly nominated, for all the offices, by the informal ballot, with space for possible changes.

These ballots having been distributed, each voter erases the names she does not want, leaving the name she chooses, or writing in still another, being careful to vote for only one person for each office. Or, if preferred, and so voted, the " Australian system " can be used, instead of the foregoing method by erasure. The ballots are then prepared as shown on the following page.

The voter then simply marks a cross against the name of the person for whom she wishes to vote; she does not erase anything, *i.e.*: —

Mrs. C. E. Burns.	
Miss J. F. Fisher.	**X**

Discussion of the claims of candidates upon the consideration of the meeting are in order at any time before the balloting begins.

THE BALLOT.

FOR PRESIDENT.	
MRS. C. E. BURNS.	
MISS J. F. FISHER.	
FOR VICE-PRESIDENT.	
MRS. A. J. HANSON.	
MRS. L. M. JACOBS.	

Another way of nominating officers is to appoint a nominating committee and to instruct them to bring in two or three names for each office instead of one name, the election then being by ballot, by means of either of the two foregoing methods.

If a meeting at which officers are elected is adjourned over until another day, to complete its business, the outgoing officers continue in power at such adjourned meeting. The in-coming officers are notified of their election by the retiring corresponding secretary, and assume their duties at the meeting following their election, unless otherwise provided in the by-laws.

To Section 34. — If the chairman does not know the name of the person who rises and "addresses the chair," she says: "What name?" The name is given, and the chairman then "recognizes" her by repeating it, and she then "has the floor."

To Section 44. — Jefferson's manual defines the limits of personality in debate, as follows: "The consequences of a measure may be reprobated in strong terms, but to arraign the motives of those who propose or advocate it is a personality and against order."

If the debater wishes to speak to any member, she does so "through the chair," saying: "Mrs. Chairman, through you, I will say to the member, etc."

To Sections 55 *and* 57. — There is a conflict of opinions upon the use of the previous question, and upon whether it is debatable. Cushing and Warrington authorize the previous question as a regular procedure; that is, it is to be used unless there is a special rule prohibiting it. The former declares it debatable unless debate is prohibited by rule; the latter, by implication, recommends a limited debate. Robert and Waples do not allow the previous question unless it is called for by a two-thirds vote; both declare it undebatable. Fish says it is undebatable. Crocker does not allow the previous question except by special rule, and when so allowed, he recommends a limited debate. With such differences of opinion among authorities, the author has been forced to choose what seems to her to be the best usage. The following is therefore recommended: —

1. The previous question is now so well established, and it

is such a safeguard against interminable debate, that it should be admitted as a part of the regular procedure and not require a special rule. (For the result of its non-use, see the proceedings of the United States Senate, 53d Congress, 1st session).

2. The possible abuse of the motion to close debate should be guarded against. The simplest and fairest way to secure this would seem to be to allow the motion for the previous question to be debated; since thereby the opponents of closing debate can speak in protest and thus prevent undue haste in coming to a vote upon the main question. Again, while it may be necessary in *legislatures* to require that the motion to close debate shall be demanded by a two-thirds vote, there is no good reason, in ordinary assemblies, for setting aside the majority principle in this instance.

3. Since there is nothing to say upon the previous question, except why or why not the "main question should now be voted upon," the debate upon the previous question is necessarily limited, and should not exceed ten minutes. It may be well to repeat that the debate upon the main question is suspended as soon as the previous question is *moved;* that such debate cannot be resumed until the motion for the previous question is decided, and that it cannot be resumed at all, unless that motion is decided in the negative.

ILLUSTRATION.

Mrs. Allen. I move the previous question.

The Chair. The previous question is moved. Shall the main question be now put? Debate of the motion for the previous question is now in order.

Mrs. Burns. I think we have not sufficiently considered this important matter, and hope the motion to close debate will not prevail.

Miss Lovell. And *I* think we have spent time enough on it, and hope we shall not discuss it any longer.

Mrs. Carter. It is much to be regretted, Mrs. President, that our townspeople have not been more generous in their responses to the call for aid from —

The Chair (interrupting). The member must proceed in order. Discussion of the *main question* is not now in order — only the motion to *close debate* is now before us. Is there any further discussion of the previous question? If not, those in favor of closing debate and coming to an immediate vote upon the question of furnishing our new hospital will say aye * * * It is a vote, and the previous question is ordered. Those now in favor of the motion "that our club subscribe $50.00 for furnishing the new city hospital," will say aye * * *

If the motion had been lost, the chair would say instead: "The motion for the previous question is lost, and the main question is still before you for discussion."

To Section 64. — In putting a motion to vote in large assemblies, it is well for the chair before "declaring" the vote, to say, "It appears to be [or not to be] a vote." Then, after a short pause, to declare the vote, saying, "It is [or is not] a vote." The declaration may be enforced by a blow of the gavel.

To Section 79. Applying this principle to the meetings of women's clubs and similar organizations, it follows that the motion to reconsider may be made at the same meeting at which the vote is passed, or at the next meeting following, where business is done. Meetings where no business is done would not be counted. Of course a vote can be reconsidered only by the same organization as that which passed it. For instance, the directors cannot reconsider a vote passed by the whole club, or *vice versa*. This is not saying, however, that a club cannot *annul* action taken by its directors.

To Section 87. Changes in words which do not affect the *sense*, are not amendments, properly speaking; that is, they do not *require* a motion to amend, though such motion, is not prohibited. The secretary, in recording a motion, may put it into better shape verbally, subject to approval at the next meeting. When there is any doubt in regard to the wording of a motion, it is best for the mover to submit it in writing. *See section 32.*.

To Section 91. — The illustration in the text is of primary and secondary amendment by *inserting;* the following are illustrations of amendment by (1) striking out, and (2) by striking out and inserting : —

1. *Motion :* that the club establish a library of books, magazines and newspapers.

Primary amendment : to strike out the words " magazines and newspapers " so that the motion would read : " a library of books."

Secondary amendment : to strike out the word " magazines " (from the primary amendment) so that the amendment would read : " to strike out the word " newspapers " only, leaving the original motion, if amended, to read : " a library of books and magazines."

The question first comes on the secondary amendment, to strike out the word " magazines " from the primary amendment, and if this prevails, then the question comes upon the primary amendment, as amended, which is to strike out the word " newspapers." Finally, the vote is taken on the " motion as amended," which is, to establish a " library of books and magazines." Of course, if the secondary amendment is *rejected*, the primary remains as originally moved; so with the original motion, if the primary is rejected.

2. *Motion:* that the club establish a library of books, magazines and newspapers.

Primary amendment: to strike out the word " newspapers " and insert the word " pamphlets," so that the motion would read: " a library of books, magazines and pamphlets."

Secondary Amendment: To strike out the word " pamphlets " and insert the words " art posters," so that the primary amendment would read " to strike out the word ' newspapers ' (from the original motion) and insert the word ' art posters.' " The question is first upon " art posters " in place of " pamphlets " and then (if this prevails) upon " art posters " in place of " newspapers," and finally, upon " a library of books, magazines and art posters."

Besides the three ways which are illustrated, there are a number of other ways in which a primary amendment may be amended secondarily, as shown by the following formula:—

MOTION: A B C D.

Primary Amendment by Inserting: To insert E F. This may be amended secondarily by (1) inserting G, so that the primary amendment, if amended, would read : " to insert E F G;" (2) striking out F, so that the primary would read: " to insert E;" (3) striking out F and inserting G so that the primary would read: " to insert E G."

Primary Amendment by Striking out: To strike out B C. This may be amended secondarily by (1) inserting D [*something from the original motion*], so that the primary would read: " to strike out B C D;" (2) striking out C, so that the primary would read: " to strike out B;" (3) striking out C and inserting D, so that the primary would read: " to strike out B D."

Primary Amendment by Striking out and Inserting: To

strike out B C, and insert E F. This may be amended secondarily by (1) inserting G, so that the primary would read: " to strike out B C, and insert, E F G;" (2) striking out F, so that the primary would read: " to strike out B C, and insert E;" (3) inserting D, so that the primary would read: "to strike out B C D, and insert E F;" (4) striking out C, so that the primary would read: " to strike out B and insert E F."

The primary amendment to strike out and insert may also be amended secondarily by *striking out and inserting on one motion*, but the illustrations of these forms would be confusing rather than helpful.

In putting the motion to vote the question is *first* upon the secondary, *second* upon the primary as amended by the secondary, and *third* upon the motion as finally amended. For instance, taking the foregoing illustration, numbered 4, the question comes *first* upon the motion to amend the amendment by striking out C (from B C) and if this prevails, *second*, upon the amendment as amended, which is to strike out B and insert E F, and if this prevails, *third*, upon the motion as amended, which would then be: A E F D.

RULES.

I. A motion " to amend by inserting " may itself be amended by inserting new words into the words to be inserted; by striking out words from the words to be inserted; and by striking out words from the words to be inserted and inserting new words in their place.

II. A motion " to amend by striking out " may itself be amended by inserting more words *from the original motion* into the words to be stricken out; by striking out words from the words to be stricken out; and by striking out words from the words to be stricken out and inserting more words from the original motion in their place.

III. A motion "to amend by striking out and inserting" may itself be amended by inserting new words into, or by striking words from, the words to be inserted; by inserting more words from the original motion into, or by striking words from, the words to be stricken out; and by combining two of these corresponding propositions into one motion "to strike out and insert."

To Article II. of By-Laws. — Honorary members have no duties, but (unless otherwise provided by special rule) are entitled to the privileges of the club without payment of the membership fee. They have no vote, but they can take part in debate unless it is voted otherwise. The office of "honorary president" is not to be commended, since it involves possible complications. Any one whom it is desired to honor would better be made an honorary vice-president or simply an honorary member. Honorary offices are simply "honors;" they confer no *rights* — of presiding, etc.

To Article V. of the By-Laws. — A constitution and by-laws should be so carefully drawn as to avoid frequent amendment if possible. But, on the other hand, they *may* be amended *ad infinitum*, until they are in the desired shape. Notice of an amendment must specifically state, in writing, the proposed change: *i. e.* Mrs. —— offers the following amendment: to strike out from Article —— of the by-laws, the words —— and to insert in their place the following words: ——, so that the article as amended would read ——

When the proper time comes (in the order of business a proposed amendment comes under the head of "special assignments,") the President reads, or causes to be read, the proposed amendment, which is then open for consideration. The mover usually opens the discussion, which is then continued like that of any other question.

The offered amendment *is itself the main question*, and it may be amended primarily and secondarily. Such primary or secondary amendments require no previous notice, but must be strictly germane; they also require only a majority vote, while the final adoption of the proposed amendment, as perfected, should require a two-thirds vote. This final vote upon the proposition to amend settles the question, and the constitution or by-law is thus amended, no further vote being required upon "the article so amended," such article not being before the meeting.

When several amendments are before the meeting, they take precedence in the order moved, unless otherwise voted. Amendments come into force as soon as adopted. They must be properly recorded, not only in the record of the meeting, but in the book containing the written constitution and by-laws.

When it is desired to make many revisions in a constitution and by-laws, a committee may be appointed, by a majority vote, to "revise the constitution and by-laws." This committee may be instructed in any way, and their report, (coming up under the head of "reports of special committees") is acted upon like the report of any other committee. *See section 134.*

Unless otherwise instructed, a committee must include, in its revision, the substance of all the provisions contained in the matter committed. If any of these were omitted, and if it is desired to retain them, they must be added, by amendment, when the revision is under consideration, by the assembly.

When this proposed revision (of the constitution or by-laws, or both,) comes up for consideration, such revision is the main question, and each proposed change therein is an amendment, which may be amended secondarily. All changes should require a two-thirds vote. Any other amendments may be made, and then a final vote is taken upon the "Constitution (or by-laws) as amended," this being decided by a majority vote. *See section 113.*

The existing constitution and by-laws are in force until the new ones are adopted as a whole.

When any contingency arises which is not provided for in these instruments, or not covered by the parliamentary authority, a club will take a vote as to what to do for the time being, and afterward, if the matter is of sufficient importance, will provide for similar contingencies in its by-laws.

It may be well to repeat:

1. By a unanimous vote an assembly may temporarily suspend any rule.

2. By a motion and a majority vote, an assembly may do any business which is not prohibited by its constitution and by-laws.

3. When parliamentary errors have been inadvertently made in the past, it is best to abide by them, and to proceed correctly in the future, rather than to try to retrace steps and correct such errors. Anything to which no objection is raised *at the time*, is presumed to have been correct.

INDEX

Among the organizations which have already adopted the *Woman's Manual* as their authority may be mentioned: —

THE GENERAL FEDERATION OF WOMEN'S CLUBS.
THE MAINE STATE FEDERATION OF WOMEN'S CLUBS.
THE IOWA FEDERATION OF WOMEN'S CLUBS.
THE KENTUCKY FEDERATION OF WOMEN'S CLUBS.
THE NEW JERSEY FEDERATION OF WOMEN'S CLUBS.
THE NEW YORK FEDERATION OF WOMEN'S CLUBS AND SOCIETIES.
THE MASSACHUSETTS FEDERATION OF WOMEN'S CLUBS.
THE NEBRASKA FEDERATION OF WOMEN'S CLUBS.
THE BUSINESS LEAGUE OF AMERICA.
THE DAUGHTERS OF THE REVOLUTION, MASSACHUSETTS.
THE WARREN AND PRESCOTT CHAPTER, D. A. R., BOSTON.
THE DAUGHTERS OF NEW HAMPSHIRE.
THE ILLINOIS WOMEN'S PRESS ASSOCIATION.
THE NEW ENGLAND WOMEN'S PRESS ASSOCIATION.
THE SAN FRANCISCO FEDERATION OF WOMEN.
THE CONNECTICUT WOMAN SUFFRAGE ASSOCIATION.
THE COLORADO EQUAL SUFFRAGE ASSOCIATION.
THE COOK COUNTY (ILL.) WOMAN SUFFRAGE ASSOCIATION.
THE FEDERAL SUFFRAGE ASSOCIATION.
THE SUPREME GRAND CHAPTER OF THE P. E. O. SISTERHOOD.
THE WOMEN'S LITERARY UNION OF PORTLAND, ME.
THE MANCHESTER, N. H., FEDERATION OF WOMEN'S CLUBS.
THE NEW CENTURY CLUB, WILMINGTON, DEL.
THE WOMAN'S CLUB, MARSHALLTOWN, IOWA.
THE WOMAN'S CLUB, CONCORD, N. H.
THE SPOKANE (WASH.) SOROSIS.
THE OSSOLI CIRCLE, KNOXVILLE, TENN.
THE WOMAN'S CLUB, LOUISVILLE, KY.
THE WOMEN'S WHEEL AND ATHLETIC CLUB, BUFFALO, N.Y.
THE WOMEN'S LITERARY CLUB, IRVING PARK, ILL.
THE LITERARY SOCIETY, BRYAN, OHIO.
THE PHIDIAN ART CLUB, DIXON, ILL.
THE WOMAN'S CLUB, SEYMOUR, CONN.
THE COLLEGE HILL PROGRESS CLUB, OHIO.
THE UNIVERSALIST LADIES' AID SOCIETY, SPOKANE, WASH.
THE FORTNIGHTLY, WINCHESTER, MASS.
THE CANTABRIGIA, CAMBRIDGE, MASS.
THE OLD AND NEW OF MALDEN, MASS.
THE MELROSE WOMAN'S CLUB, MASS.
THE FRIDAY CLUB, EVERETT, MASS.
THE YOUNG WOMEN'S CLUB, LYNN, MASS.
THE ABBOT ACADEMY CLUB, MASS.
THE DORCHESTER WOMAN'S CLUB, MASS.
THE DANVERS WOMEN'S ASSOCIATION, MASS.
MARY A. LIVERMORE CHAPTER, LYCEUM LEAGUE OF AMERICA, MALDEN MASS.
THE BOSTON POLITICAL CLASS — AND MANY OTHERS.

www.ingramcontent.com/pod-product-compliance
Lightning Source LLC
Chambersburg PA
CBHW031407270326
41929CB00010BA/1364